A TENACIOUS JOURNEY OF ACHIEVING A LIFE OF PURPOSE!

BELIEVE is so wonderfully written – the reader is captivated from page one! Being propelled into this humble journey of impoverished beginnings to newfound glory, and the perseverance of hope and faith along the way is powerful. Believe exemplifies the road map and building blocks in life of a young woman striving for more, all while portraying the importance of giving unto others and believing the good you outpour in life comes back full circle. No matter the circumstance, true happiness is found in gratefulness and giving back.

Dr. Donna Barrett is so well versed in painting a vivid story that every reader will find themselves on an emotional journey filled with tears, laughter, joy, and fullness. This is a light, yet deeply moving read, which accelerates the reader's eagerness to continue further to see how the story unfolds.

The prologue of this book teaches us to look at life with a glass half full mentality; to always share our riches with those less fortunate and lend a helping hand to every neighbor in need, as not all surrounding us are as fortunate. That no matter the curveballs life throws our way, with the right attitude, prayer, and belief, good things will come.

I cannot think of one reader who will not benefit from picking up a copy of this book and taking a moment to reflect within; Dr. Barrett's brilliance is captivating and reminds us with a determined mind, no achievement is short of possible. No matter where we are headed in this journey of life, we must always circle back to our roots and remember where we came from to preserve our humility. Most importantly, the reader is reminded that anything is possible with just a morsel of belief. —**Embar Adika**

~

Experience turned into brilliance! Dr. Barrett takes you through her experiences with an interesting flavor. She shares precious moments where God has worked wonders in her life. God bless these amazingly inspiring words!" —**Georgia Alvaranga**

~

What a riveting and captivating life example of resiliency saturated with strength unfolding line per line; all guided by the Most High God!

Through the pages of this text it is clear, Dr. Donna exemplified blind trust and faith that God will prevail every time...and HE did!" —**Elaine M. Barclay, Ph.D., LPC, NBCC, THTC, HS-BCP**

~

Donna Barrett is an authentic hard worker and robust achiever whose faith in God and supportive goodwill to people lead her to success. Donna is admired for her candid prowess in overcoming intense obstacles and potentially dangerous situations on the journey of life. We do not only share her most private experiences, but in her recognition of wonderful people in her circle. I strongly recommend the author and her work. I hope that as you read it you may, like her, set sail knowing that "Whatever the mind can conceive, it can achieve." —**Sandra Fletcher, EdD**

~

Dr. Donna Barrett has an inspiring story to tell. It is about God's providential leading in her life and her willingness to faithfully follow where He leads. Although the path sometimes seems obscured, she declares, "My roots are humble yet significant." The significance of this book is inescapably tied to the author's humble beginning. Her life story paints an interesting picture, a kaleido-scope of events that are integral to her present success as a: church leader, wife, mother, entrepreneur, philanthropist and university lecturer. This book will help the reader to be mentally prepared for adversity, to refuse giving up when crisis comes, to cultivate a spirit of determination and to believe absolutely in God's promises to take care of His children. —**Pastor C. Norman Harding**

We have waited and now it is here! Believe is such an inspiration to all of us. Dr. Donna's book highly speaks of the power of believing that anything is possible. Her story touches your heart and encourages you to follow your dreams through three foundational principles: faith, hope, and belief. This is a must read that will transform your life! —**Delbon Johnson**

Believe demonstrates that Donna is:

Determined and intentional
Overcomer of obstacles
Never ceasing in her quest to constantly move upward
Never ending in her love for God, her family, and others
Achiever of goals and successful

From the first day we met until now, Donna has been the epitome of her name. Believe will inspire you to continue moving upwards, onwards and forward walking in your God-given purpose. —**Debra Johnson-King, MBA, CPC**

One can hardly give the merited appreciation to Dr. Donna Barrett's sublime glory, unless they know her enthralling story, in which she has labored to transform the humble beginnings, imperiled by fears and hardship to nobler purposes. Though early fettered by anguish, hard work and academic prerogatives have taken her from the below deck experience, to surf upon the waves of life's tempestuous circumstances.

In her Book, BELIEVE which highlights her journey from Nassau port to America, Dr. Barret has cogently preserved the memory of her pensive ocean dilemma, which like the Bible's Jonah, she writhe anxiously below the deck of a ship on her journey to America. Unlike the reluctant prophet, she was to avoid having a 'whale of a time.' The unexpurgated events of her life are here showcased, placed on display, none more enthralling than her stowaway experience, framed with a retrospective relevance, exquisitely told and grippingly transmitted to print.

The book, a must read, is a repository of her personal, emotional and psychological artifacts, a collection of prime events, documented facts, and an inspiration of which she credits the Creator for her overcoming. Therein, literary aficionados, with specks perched on their noses, dazed by her courage, will most certainly find this book a true classic, punctuated by moments of serious musings, and tacit laughter, in which her experience will hang on the gallery of the reader's thoughts.

Indeed, the poignancy of Dr. Barrett's narrated struggles along the journey, invokes inquisitive wonderment, and cheers, a wow experience! The pages of this book are crowded with enough intrigues and admiration to hold the reader's attention, to the end, inexorably link to her sanctified afflictions and redemptive successes. —**Dr. Desmond A. Mattocks**

Believe

A TENACIOUS JOURNEY OF ACHIEVING A LIFE OF PURPOSE!

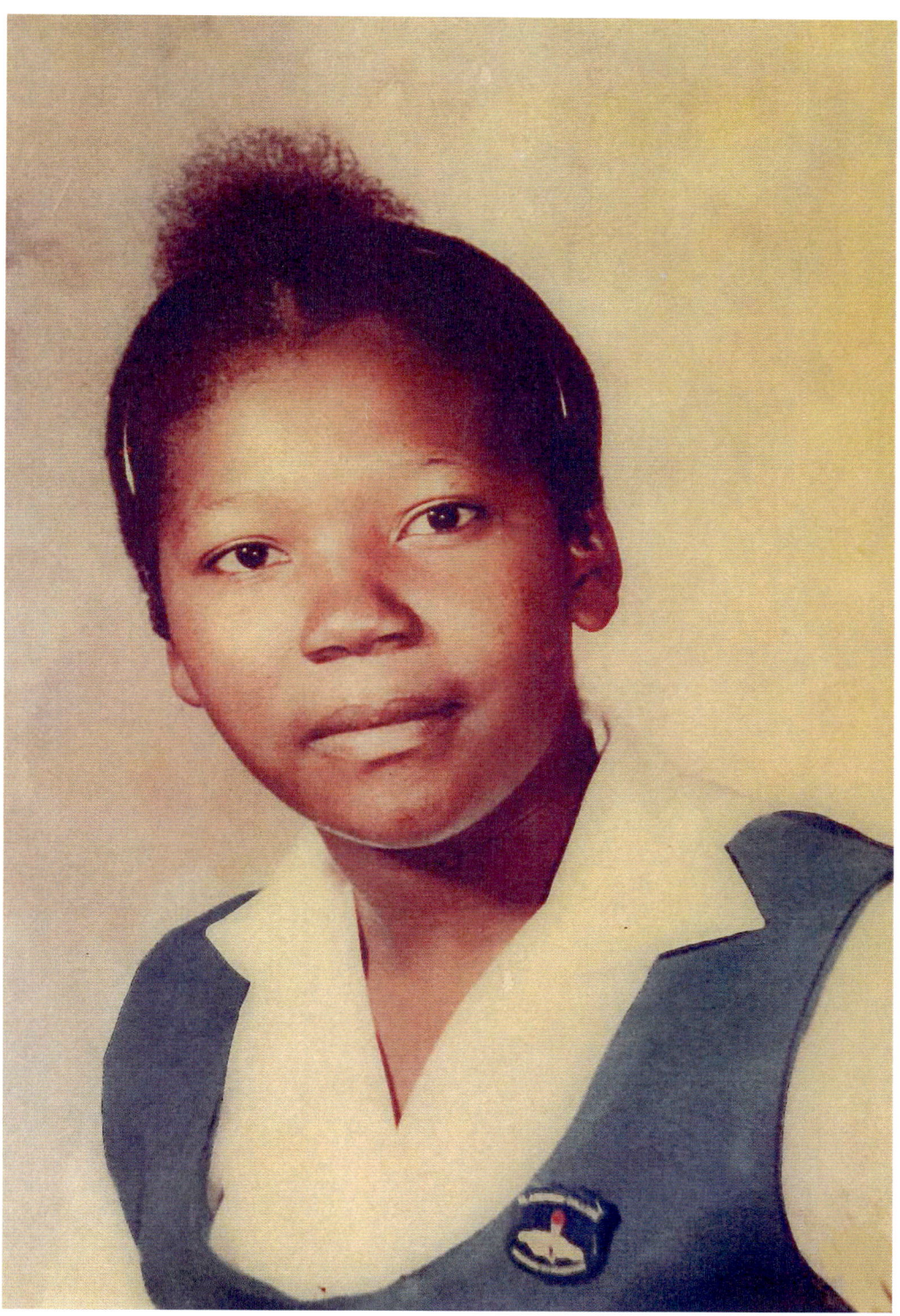

BELIEVE

A Tenacious Journey of Achieving a Life of Purpose!

DR. DONNA BARRETT

Write The Vision Creative Works,LLC

Write The Vision Creative Works,LLC

Believe: A Tenacious Journey of Achieving a Life of Purpose!
Published by: Write The Vision Creative Works, LLC
PO Box 390661, Snellville, GA 30039
Writethevisioncreativeworks.com

Editing, Writing Services & Cover Design: Write The Vision Creative Works, LLC

Photography: All Photos Provided by Dr. Donna Barrett

Library of Congress Control Number: 2020921837

ISBN: 978-0-578-79247-7 (WTVCW)
ISBN: 9798700180719   (Amazon)

I dedicate this book to my loving husband, Philip, for his untiring support in everything I do. I also dedicate this book to my three beautiful daughters: Kameisha, Nekeisha, and Chante' who understood from an early age, "If you believe, you will achieve," and have been successful in their chosen careers. Additionally, I dedicate this book to everyone who acknowledges, "Anything is possible when you believe!"

Foreword

When I met my wife, Donna, it was evident to me that she was, *and still is*, an ambitious woman. After we married, I began to see her work hard to accomplish her dreams, and I was very supportive. I've heard about some men who have issues with their wives accomplishing their goals. Not me. I didn't mind if she had more education than me. I thought, "The higher the education she has, the better for us. The more money she makes, I make."

So, I was just as motivated as she was when she decided to go back to school and left her jobs. I also had a decent job working at the post office so I knew we would be fine. I recognized when a job stressed my wife and I wanted the stress off her. My mindset is if the job is not for you, move on. So, when she left stressful jobs behind, I was happy for her. I was happy for us!

Once she wanted to help her brother get his business off the ground, and she was gone for a year. I supported it. I told her, "Go check it out and see what it is."

It didn't bother me. One of our daughters was in college and two were in high school. So, they were able to do a lot on their own. Mostly, I would just go to work and come back. And of course, I would take care of what was needed. Donna and I talked a lot on the phone during that season. It wasn't really that stressful. I was able to manage it. Everything she does, I support.

Donna always knows what she wants, and whatever goal she wants to achieve, she goes for it! When she was working on her Ph.D., she would get up at night while I was sleeping upstairs. Oh man! I wouldn't do that, but I have always admired my wife's determination.

She won't give up. She doesn't know how to give up. She says, "I gotta go. I gotta push forward. Don't say I can't do it." That's the word in the family, "Don't say I can't, don't say, I don't know how to do it." Even if it's hard, try hard enough and you will be successful.

Her work ethic has even inspired me to pursue my goals. One time I was saying, "No, I am not going to finish my degree."

She said, "Yes, you can do it. Do it!"

It was important. And I finished my degree! As you read, be determined. Know, anything you want to do, you can do. You've just *gotta* have faith. Trust and just do it.

Donna came under the ship and now she is on top of the ship! And she's still *moving on up!* As you read about how Donna reached from point A to point B and you come to know how she got from there to here, know it is possible for you to achieve your goals too! If she can do it, so can you.

Remember, with a little time and effort —even in marriage, you just *have* to trust. You and the people God has called you to do life with, should always help each other — it's teamwork. One can't go right while the other goes left. You must go together. Over the years, Donna and I have learned to sit down, plan something and we always come to an agreement. This is necessary for it all to work together. It can't work if your team is out of sync. If there is disagreement, the team will not win. Take from this, in all business, you must keep focus. As you read *Believe*, it is important to surround yourself with people who will support you as you pursue your dreams.

— Philip Barrett, *Husband*

My mom is a very God-fearing woman. She's very passionate – with her heart, soul and mind – about everything she does. Whether it be work, taking care of us or being a wife. God is in the center of everything. Mom is dedicated and a hard worker. Mommy is very kind, giving, and she has an impeccable heart. She came into a country where all you heard was, "America is the land of the free," not knowing if it would be true for herself. Received by my Uncle Robert and his family, she took a huge step of faith to journey here. She arrived, learned how to live out her dreams, all while taking care of us. Even though my sisters and I are now grown, she still looks out for us. She comforts us. She loves us. She always gives her wisdom and teaching. The message she lives by, "If you believe, you can achieve anything you put your mind to, with having God in the center," has always stuck with me. I think this was instilled in her as a little kid by her parents.

I don't know how Mommy does it sometimes. She's always on the go. She owns her own business, HomeValue Group. She serves as elder at her church. She plans church activities and attends about three or four times a week. If you call Mommy, she will drop everything she's doing to be by your side. She'll work it out some way. Her love for her children is like none other. She is truly the best mom ever!

She came to the U.S. and didn't have anything. From the bottom of the ship to where she is now! From a GED to a Ph.D. – Her story is amazingly inspiring! Her cheerful, happy and outgoing spirit has been duplicated in my daughter, Madison, and I consider this to be a tremendous gift. If you can glean an inkling of the love my Mommy pours out to others from reading this book, your life will be impacted for the better! Even through her struggles, like the deaths of her brothers, sister, mom, and dad; she has still managed to rise to the top. The message of her life is important. This book is a vehicle to portray that message. Grab hold to it, believing you can achieve and carry God with you through it all.

—Kameisha Johnson, First Born

As a child, I remember my mom working. She's always balanced work, family, and spiritual life. I've seen her on the go, and consistently trying to achieve something better. She often says, "If you believe, you will achieve." Since I was a child, I've seen her motivated to do more. I recall even when she went back to school. She was never not around or not involved because or her educational pursuits. She was always there.

As we got much older, she would be up late at night working on papers for her doctorate, and she included us in the process by inviting us to read. Many people make goals and get sidetracked. Not Mommy. She remains focused despite obstacles. I know this is why my sisters and I always strive to accomplish our goals.

Almost everything I've done is due to my faith in God and from being inspired by my parents. When I went to nursing school, I had my son, and felt like there was absolutely no way I would be able to do both. My mom said, "Yes, you can – don't say you can't. Never say you can't." Thankfully, I continued, and I kept focused. I wouldn't be where I am today without my mother's positive influence. I'm proud of everything she has done.

As you read, Believe, know there will be obstacles and things that get in the way on your journey. Even things you feel you cannot do. Know if you keep the faith, pray, and manage your time well, you can reach your goals! Many people think about what they want to do, and they never take the first step. Mom, has instilled the alternative, the ability to do into her children and grandchildren instead. Now, you too can glean from her wisdom.

—Nekeisha Basko, Second Born

Honestly, I don't even know how she did it all – raising my two sisters and me. All I remember is going to school as a little kid and mom waking up extra early, usually 4:30 every morning. She would be seated in the same spot with her laptop open, researching and writing. She would wake up before all of us, and she would be the last person to go to sleep. She did that with perseverance and consistency. That's what I admire about her! Throughout the entire period of getting her Ph.D, many things were happening within our family, including her sister and her brother's death. It was a lot for her to take in altogether. As I said before, I don't know how she was able to do everything, but she persevered, and I admire her for it.

I know it wasn't easy at all. She could have given up so many times. She could have thrown in the towel. But she didn't. There was a particular time when she had to go out of town to take care of my brother-in-law, as he was in and out of the hospital. She said, "Yes, I'm going to be there," took her laptop with her and finished her assignments. It was like nothing was stopping her or in her way. She does not use excuses. She remains diligent, despite obstacles, and this is exactly how she pursues the path before her.

If you meet her, trust me, you're going to find another mother. She's the type of person who automatically accepts you as family from the very beginning, upon first meeting. She has a very caring and very loving heart. She always wants to help no matter what the situation is. She will go over and beyond for a person she barely even knows. Honestly, I have so many friends personally, and so do my sisters, who view my mom as a second mom to them. If we needed to open up the door to anybody in any situation, my mom would be the first one to help. Because of her character, a lot of people call on her.

Mom has passed her love and reverence for God down to her daughters and family. As spiritual mom to many, she sets a positive example. As an adult I am coming to understand what it's like to live in this world and to go through challenges. These experiences have provided great insight on everything my mom sacrificed to get where she is now. I see the tenacity behind all her endeavors. Just her story of coming from the bottom of the ship to arrive here required sacrifice and faith in God. Like both of my parents, I too am, in real estate and as a result, I'm gleaning even more of Mom's wisdom in this field. I really didn't realize how much my parents sacrificed for us when I was a child. Now, having grown up, and observing my sisters as mothers, I get it. I know for a fact, my mom paved the way for all of us. It is because of her that we are where we are today. It is my prayer that you read Believe and be blessed.

— Chante' Barrett, Third Born

Donna is a phenomenal woman, mother, sister-friend, and counselor. I can tell you from my experience with my sister, she has been there for me through thick and thin and never asks for anything in return. If she couldn't help me, she would find someone who could. She is resilient, she's tenacious, she is loving, she is kind, she is forgiving, she's successful, she is wonderful, and she will always mentor you. I went through cancer, and she was there by my side through it all. Because of her, I was able to stand strong and battle cancer. God is her foundation, and because she has a good foundation with God, she can withstand every situation coming against her. She's a strong woman, and I love her very much. She is kind, gentle, very active with our church, and she loves God. When we were growing up, she was always one of those who never said anything ill of anyone. She always listened to our mother and father or anyone older than her. She never gave trouble - she was always the one listening and helping people. She is the matriarch of our family. If our family is going through any crisis, she will be the one who steps in and walks, comes alongside you, walks you through whatever you're going through, and stays with you until you overcome the situation. She means the world to me. When I talk about her, it brings tears to my eyes. Tears of joy to see her accomplishments and where she has come from. She is so resilient and tenacious; she achieved her destiny. I remember when she was completing her doctoral work, I said to her, "What are you going to do next?" She never stops. She never stops trying to reach and achieve something more. Know, her achievements, are never about her – they are always about others.

I love her very, very much! She's a woman of God, and anything she says, you can take it to the bank. If she can't do it, she'll find someone capable. That's how she is. The impact of this book will be powerful. Every challenge she has faced, she has overcome. As you read, know for sure you can, and with Jesus at the center of it all, you will overcome too.

— **Yvonne Black, Sister**

There are so many great things about Donna. She is a motivator. That's what I love about her! If she is doing something good, you can bet she will encourage you to be a part of it. I've never met anyone who encourages you to do better, be better, and try to encourage others the way she does. I can say after finishing her first class, she called me and said, "Maryse, I just started my Ph.D. program." I thought, "Okay." She said, "I called the advisor, and he is going to call you." I said, "What? What am I going to do in a Ph.D. program?" And then, after the advisor called me, I said, "Donna, what are we going to do?" She encouraged me and told me so many great things we could do together.

Now, I can say we've started many initiatives - even in the middle of the Ph.D. program. We created an organization, Fostering Connections, Inc., when she finished her first chapter. She started the organization, and afterwards, she said, "You know what? Let's start, Inspired by Love." I don't know where she comes up with these ideas. Since we started Inspired by Love, we've been trying to help people from other countries. Whenever we meet, she always has new ideas and says, "We're going to do this!"

I see her daughters. They follow her footsteps. They love to encourage others, just like her. I call her my sister because I remember when my sister passed five years ago, we were right in the middle of writing our dissertations. I said, "You know what, I just don't know what to do." She told me, "Okay, just sit down." That simple advice was just what I needed. If I didn't have her, I don't think I would be able to stand up to do anything.

Even during our Ph.D. program, we always called it a journey. During this journey, we climbed mountains. We walked in the valley. When we first started, she lost a sister, which was my sister too, because I knew Sister Jean very well. Then she called and said, "I don't think I can deal with this program anymore." I encouraged her, and I said, "No, you got me into this, we're going to do it together." Just as when I said, "I want to take a pause, I want to give up," she said, "No, you're not going to leave me to walk by myself." We became motivators for each other. When she's discouraged, I encourage her. When I'm discouraged, she encourages me. Together, we walked the path of our Ph.D. program, just a couple months apart from each other. She was there for me, and I'm always going to be there for her.

When she first told me how she came to America, I said, "What? You came to America by boat, Donna?" She got her GED, and now she has a Ph.D. To me, this speaks volumes for everybody.

The world is limitless, as long as you put your mind to it, and as long as you determine you can go places.

God allowed her to walk this path and I always tell her she is the sister I never had. People sometimes see us when we go to Jamaica together and always say, "We didn't know you had another sister." She always says, "Yes, I have another sister." One beautiful thing I can say is she's all together loving – a loving person. Meeting at church, our children grew up together. It's like we walked a path, up mountains and valleys. We are always by each other's side. Today, even when we speak casually, I refer to her as Dr. Barrett because I know what it means to accomplish this goal. Now, we walk the path so we can open other avenues for others.

Believe will inspire many. She starts everything with love. Not only with love, but she starts everything with the love her parents instilled in her. She always tells me her parents said, if you don't have education, then you cannot accomplish good things in life. I tell her my parents always told me the same thing. Maybe that's what bonded us together. Believe, whatever you are and wherever you are, you need to keep moving on. As long as you're breathing, keep walking. Keep walking because your life is not over.

— Dr. Maryse Desir, Spiritual Sister & Friend

Acknowledgments

First and foremost, I give all praise and glory to God for being my Rock, my Shield, and a very present help in times of trouble. His everlasting mercies, His renewed grace, and unconditional love is unmatched. They have kept me grounded in my faith and allowed me to maintain a steadfast gaze on my goals and dreams.

I remain confident in His amazing promises: "...I will never leave you nor forsake you" (Hebrews 13:5b ESV), "For I know the plans I have for you, declares the Lord, plans to prosper you and not to harm you, plans to give you hope and a future." (Jeremiah 29:11 NIV), and "I hereby command you: Be strong and courageous; do not be frightened or dismayed, for the Lord your God is with you wherever you go," (Joshua 1:9 NRSV).

As I reflect on my life, I reflect on my journey from Jamaica to the Bahamas to the United States. My longing for higher education, the desire to use my God-given talents for my career, and my loving family were the driving force that propelled me to achieve what the Lord had instructed me to do.

However, my family played a huge part in getting me where I

am today. On my ship of life, these are the passengers who have journeyed along with me:

My Parents

I admired the love my parents shared for one another. On their 37th wedding anniversary, my siblings and I arranged for them to renew their vows. We all flew to Jamaica for the ceremony. It was a warm and sunny day. We captured a picture of my parents standing outside the church. While holding Mama's hand, Papa was also looking into the camera with his serious face and a demeanor of a hardworking man. Mama was showing off her warm smile, radiating in her white dress with a veiled cap on her head flowing down to her low-heeled pumps. The photo was a close reflection of their four decades of love and dedication to each other.

Living in separate countries did not stop us from remaining close. After I left Jamaica, Mama and Papa moved from our child-hood home in Clarendon to Mandeville, which was next door to my brother, Kenneth. The move had been Kenneth's idea to keep Mama and Papa safe from the violent political fighting erupting during this time. Papa retired from the taxi job in Mandeville when he reached 60 and took up farming. He was passionate about farm-ing. And he loved taking care of all sorts of animals. Papa never sold any of his crops. Instead, he neatly packaged and gave them to family and friends. He did this for many years. Then, on February 19, 2002, we faced a day filled with sorrow. My brother, Winston, called to tell me Papa had passed away. He was truly a giant in our family. Mama was heartbroken, but she handled Papa's passing with a prayerful reminder of them meeting again when Jesus returns.

Toward the end of Mama's life, she wasn't feeling her best. But even sickness could not shake her faith in God. She still began every letter she wrote with the phrase, "Greetings in the mighty name of Jesus." She ended each with, "Continue to trust in the

Lord with all your might." She and I stayed very close, whether I was visiting in Jamaica or if she was spending time with my family in Florida. Our favorite pastime was her entertaining us with her childhood stories. She always reminded us to stand firm in our faith. Another sorrowful day came on July 11, 2010, when we said goodbye to Mama at the Mandeville Public Hospital. Although, both Papa and Mama are no longer with us, I will always be thankful of the first two people who showed me how great faith in God should be carried out.

My Husband

A big thank you to my loving husband, Philip, for always being my loudest cheerleader, strongest supporter, and devoted father. He is the wind beneath my wings and the anchor in my waves. I am filled with appreciation for the care and love he has shown over the last 38 years and continues to show even now. His belief that I had the ability to pursue my educational goals was evident when he took me for a surprise ride that cool and blissful spring morning to the campus of Miami Dade Community College. The words, "anything is possible when you believe," are forever etched in my mind. His encouragement was the driving force behind every class assignment, every exam, every research project, and the successful completion of my doctoral program. The sacrifices he made, the care he has shown, and the love displayed were enough to captivate my heart and change the whole trajectory of my life. Words will never be enough to express my gratitude for his support in everything I do.

My Children

To my amazing daughters: Kameisha, Nekeisha, and Chante', thank you all for the love, care, and kindness you show in both small and big ways. Each of you are a source of strength, inspiration, and courage. It amazes me that you find time to plan and execute every special day, whether it be birthday, anniversary, graduation, or holidays. Thank you for making my life rich and meaningful in every way. I could not ask for more loving, caring, and considerate daughters.

Kameisha, my firstborn, has a heart of gold. Her patience, resilience, and strong faith in God has carried her through some of the biggest challenges in her life. I am truly amazed to watch her handle life's most difficult obstacles with grit and grace. She was awarded a master's in Human Resources Management from Nova University. Today, she's a thriving human resources manager. She lives in Georgia with her husband, Delbon, and daughter, Madison.

My second daughter, Nekeisha, is a registered nurse. She completed a master's degree in Nursing Informatics at Walden University. Today, she is a remarkable case manager for a large health organization. We are super proud to call Nekeisha our family nurse. She exemplifies some of the best qualities of a nurse: caring, kind, compassionate, supportive, emphatic attitude, and detail oriented. She and her husband, Malick; son, Devon; and daughter, Laila, live in Georgia.

My youngest, Chante', is a former elementary school teacher. She earned a Bachelor of Arts degree in Elementary Education from Florida Atlantic University. She is passionate about teaching and often visits her students and volunteers when she can. Two years ago, she paused her teaching career and is now the team lead for our real estate firm (The HomeValue Group). Her compelling performance and amazing success make it an easy decision for Philip and me to pass the torch.

My hope is that my daughters and grand-children (Devon, Madison, and Laila) continue to trust in the Lord with all their heart. My desire is that they will make a positive impact on whatever capacity they are called to serve. May they continue to Believe anything is possible, and may they never forget "If you Believe, you will Achieve."

My Siblings

Special thanks to my extraordinary family! Thank you my sisters, Jean (deceased) and Yvonne; my amazing brothers, Robert, George (deceased), Noel, Winston, Kenneth, Anthony, Wayne, and Trevor (deceased) who have each played a significant part in my life. I am forever grateful for the memories we shared. I am not sure where I would be if it wasn't for their unconditional love and steadfast commitment to family. Each of my siblings has a special place in my heart.

My Extended Family and Friends

A special thanks to my family members and friends who graciously accepted the call to be interviewed for this book. Your kind words and direct contributions are a blessing. I am overjoyed to know I have made an incredible impact on your lives to the point that you have become more focused and purposeful in the belief that you can achieve anything you put your mind to.

To all my other family members and friends; too many to mention by name, thank you for being a part of my life. Each of you have possessed a profound optimism that is greatly appreciated.

To the success of The HomeValue Group, we must thank our team: Chante', Carmen, Namika, Sherry, Tashie, and Viviene; our real estate professionals. To Errol and Ronnie, our supporting staff; and Embar, Morgan, Roxy and Dennis, our amazing partners; thank you for the great relationship we have developed over the years!

Thank you to my church family at Saving Grace Seventh-day Adventist Church. Your sincere prayers for my family and me have carried us through some of the most difficult times. I am forever thankful.

A big thank you to everyone that has reviewed *Believe*: Dr. Elaine M. Barclay, Dr. Desmond A. Mattocks, Pastor Norman C.

Harding, Georgia Alvaranga, Dr. Sandra Fletcher, Debra Johnson-King, Embar Adika and Delbon Johnson.

I express my gratitude to my amazing chief executive writer and editor for stepping in at the right time with a valuable force. Their guidance, invaluable insight, excellent suggestions and passion to bring my story to life, helped steer the product to its final destination. The weekly check-in calls, the book cover design, the interviews with family members and friends, the genius idea of the *Decks* of my journey created a robust flavor for my life. I am forever grateful!

Although the writing of this book only convened the winter of 2018, the thought can be traced back over five decades ago when I realize that anything is possible if I believe. Another statement was firmly cemented when my daughters were involved in Mcknight Achievers (a program that recognized children for their academic excellence and community involvement). *If you believe, you will achieve* became my philosophy, my mantra, my commitment, and my affirmation. Reflecting on the summer job I was assigned over forty years ago was in a lot of ways the starting point to many of the qualities I have developed.

I must send a big thank you to the contributors who wrote the *Foreword* – to my husband, Philip, my daughters: Kameisha, Nekeisha, and Chante'; my sister, Yvonne, and my dear friend, Maryse. This book was in the making long before I realized and could not become a reality unless some amazing people helped shape and mold it. Their insightful feedback, genuine support, constant prayers, and encouraging words made it all possible.

Contents

Prologue

BELOW DECK: COMING TO AMERICA

*W*elcome aboard!

If this is your first time boarding a cruise, you are in for an unforgettable experience. Expect some motion as the waves of life come crashing into our ship. This journey will have its moments of uncertainty. But I can assure you, the destination will be worth the risk.

Before we depart, let's take a peek below deck.

"Down there," says the man with the blank gaze. He points to the steps leading to the lower level of the ship.

I'm confused. From the faces of the others in my group, I can tell they are confused too. We were promised a cabin with a bed before boarding the ship. Why were we being ordered to enter the ship basement?

We murmur to each other, but with caution. We can't allow our voices to rise above a whisper. It is just past midnight. We knew the ship was still docked in the Port of Nassau. If any of the guests or crew suspect we're on board, we would surely be arrested.

"Keep it moving!" said the man.

We followed his orders. Anxiously making our way downstairs, into the darkness, at the bottom of the cruise liner. The ship was strikingly beautiful outside, I'm sure no one would believe it hid a hideous cellar inside. Once downstairs, the new man in charge addresses us six *secret* travelers. I'm thinking, where is the man who took my money? I soon learned he's no longer running this operation.

We were told to be still until guests were in their cabins. Then, the man took off! Frightened and confused, we hunched over the cold iron fixtures. Our bodies were bent and unable to stand up straight. The pipes zigzagged in horizontal patterns above our heads. We were cramped. Freezing cold. I thought we could be called upstairs any moment. In my mind, I heard an imaginary clock ticking. Two hours passed before it dawned on me, "we have a two-day trip in our cramped traveling quarters. Will America be worth it?" A miserable thought, for sure. But considering all the sacrifices I've made to be here, a dozen or so more hours in the basement wasn't going to break me. Nothing would stop me from reaching my new home.

Moments passed as hours went by. Then one of our guides approached us with a startling announcement. He was cheated out of his share of the money! We paid $1500 each to ride this ship! My heart sank. He said unless he was compensated soon, he was going to report us.

The fear and worry began to thicken the atmosphere as we trembled. None of us had anything to spare – not one extra dollar to give away. A few days prior to our journey, we gave the men the full amount they requested. They assured us we were all set to go. Our only other task was to arrive at our allotted time, and we were guaranteed a spot. *Why on earth was this happening now?*

Then, a small ray of hope! I remembered the extra money in

my pocket. I was saving it to start my new life in America. It was all I had left. I made a difficult, but necessary, choice.

"I've got $200," I said. "Will that be enough?"

The man smiled. It was a look of pure satisfaction.

"Yes," he nods and grabs the cash from my hand. His scheme had worked.

My brain began to bob in and out of consciousness.

In and out.

In and out.

Then something snapped within me. *I remembered how I got over.* Mentally, I saw my mother. She relied on her spirituality to fight her battles. I knew if she were in my shoes, she would have gone deep into prayer. I closed my eyes, offered thanks to the Lord, and put my complete faith in Him. I believed the Almighty was watching over me. He would not forsake His child.

Slowly, I felt fear. It once engulfed me and now it was falling away. My tears had dried before I even sealed my prayer with an "Amen." I turned my eyes to my new friends and noticed they were praying too. Surrounded by the Lord's presence, I regained my composure. We were fine. Everything was going to be okay.

My thoughts go to scenes of America. Soon, we would have access to all the opportunities we heard so many stories about. If we could hang on a little longer, the journey would be worth it. The highs and lows of the past few weeks, still fresh in mind, would soon become memories. The dreams of making it big in a new country would soon be our reality.

I could still hear the objections of my concerned sister.

"Are you crazy? Suppose you get caught? Suppose the ship sinks? *Think of Mama and Dad!*"

I thought of my parents back in Jamaica. Admittedly, this brought a touch of guilt. Those two God-fearing people had no idea their nineteen-year-old daughter was sailing to America like cargo. But yet, I knew I must go on.

I straightened my shoulders and imagined how good it would

feel to stand up. But there was no room to even stretch my limbs. I wondered how much longer it would be. *This is crazy!* However, I knew if I wanted to make it off the ship, I had to change my temperament. It was smarter to remain calm and make the best of this hair-raising situation.

The others were silent. We sat with our arms wrapped tightly over our chests, hoping the heat from our bodies would keep us warm. I concentrated on the ship's steady strides. I tried to overlook the joyful laughter from guests watching a movie in the theater, a few floors above our heads.

More time passes before we notice the ship has stopped moving.

"Did we reach?" I whispered.

No one answers.

Several hours go by, and then a crewman comes to tell us the ship has just docked.

"We're in the Port of Miami, but none of you can leave for several hours," he said, "not until every guest has cleared immigration!"

We sat perfectly still and waited for him to return. Two hours went by before he reappeared. He gestured, "follow me." We formed a line behind him. After every four to five steps, he stopped. Then he looked around. He seemed to worry about crew members spotting us. When we entered the dining room, immigration officers were seated around a table. To my surprise, they did not seem to be startled or concerned.

We continued making our way through the empty ship. Knowing we were minutes away from stepping on American soil sent chills down my spine. My adrenaline began to rush as I imagined what it would feel like breathing the air in my new country! My excitement grew by the second.

We were just minutes away from exiting when we were stopped in our tracks by several crewmen. They were all frowning and formed a circle around us.

"What are you doing here?" an official called nearby.

I could feel the blood rush to my head. My heart felt as heavy as a cannonball.

"Show your ID!" the officer demanded.

One of the five people with me boldy responded.

"We're on the ship to visit some friends," he said.

But another man panicked. He darted to the balcony's railing and jumped overboard. I'm not sure what happened to him. The rest of us stood frozen. Afraid to move. Afraid to breathe. I pretended I was a traveler who was engrossed in my new surroundings. I grabbed my camera – which had no film – and started snapping pictures. My main goal was not to let the crewmen see me shaking like a leaf.

I had no idea whether they noticed or not. The scene unfolding before my eyes was one of pure terror. They continued to demand identification. As I tried to calm myself, I continued to snap pictures. My hands started to tremble — the voices in my head raged. *Oh Lord, what kind of ID can I possibly show them? Lord, please help me!*

Deck 1

ATRIUM: ROOTED IN JAMAICA

"When you Believe in your abilities, you change the trajectory of your life."

THE BEGINNING.

The doors opening up to the Atrium of my life reveal tender childhood memories. Jamaican waters surround me. The sun breathes life into my skin daily. The love of family and friends fill me up. I feel blessed.

My roots are humble yet significant. They are the foundation of the interior beauty of my life's story. The woman I am today would not exist without this starting point. Diving into my story begins right here.

"I am Donna Marie Precious Black," I would answer if someone asked my name.

"'*Precious*?' Where on earth did you get the name 'Precious?'" Mama would ask me with a gleam in her eye, which made me giggle.

"I don't know!" I'd say.

We would both start laughing.

The West Indies. Where it all begins.

I was born in an island paradise. A country known all over the world as the most radiant jewel of the Caribbean. Jamaica and I grew up together. Our birthdays are close. I was born August 8, 1962, just two days after the island won its independence from the British crown. I was the ninth of eleven children born to Wesley and Florence Black. Like my siblings, I wasn't born in a hospital but my parents' home.

My parents had come from Mandeville, the capital and largest town in Manchester. It is an important commercial center about 60 miles west of Kingston. Mama was born February 4, 1926, in Prattville, Manchester. Her parents were Robert Crawford and Ellen Johnston. Mama was an excellent student, but she was taken out of school after third grade to help support the family after her dad died. Later, her mother also became ill and stopped working, so Mama continued to earn a living for the family after moving in with my uncle, John. Each morning she wrapped up goods to sell, loaded them onto a donkey, and rode to the market.

Papa was born June 13, 1922, in Richmond, Christiana. His parents, Llewellyn and Ethel Black, had three boys and two girls. When he was still young, his parents died. Much like Mama, Papa was forced to leave Christiana Elementary School in search of a job in Manchester.

My parents, both hard workers, met as Papa was delivering bread to the Alley market. They fell in love and were married August 1954. Unfortunately, their first child passed of pneumonia. Coping with this loss, they decided to relocate.

Not long after their move, they were swindled out of their money by a local pastor. He misled them to believe they were depositing money towards purchasing a home in Manchester. This bad deal is what brought them to York Town in Clarendon, a parish flanked on its western side by Manchester and the east by Saint Ann. Clarendon is broad and flat; its year-round temperatures hover at ninety degrees. It's where I and some of my siblings were born and where we grew up – living in a single-story, five-bedroom home.

My parents fared well. Papa drove a taxi, and Mama took care of home. We weren't well-off, but we had more material comforts than our neighbors. My parents believed in sharing our good fortune to help others. We were the only family with a refrigerator, so Mama allowed others to use it for perishables, and we held *TV night* for our neighborhood at our home. We also took in folks who needed a place to stay. Mama took them in and shared what we had. Many would follow the scents of delicious cabbage, dumplings, yams, and callaloo from Mama's kitchen and would leave with a plate.

My parents were also dedicated members of the Seventh-day Adventist Church, one of the major denominations of the Christian religion in Jamaica. Their faith was such a big part of who they were and how they raised us. I wouldn't be exaggerating to say their religion defined them. Mama and Papa practiced their faith every single day and made sure we did too. At four o'clock every morning, Mama roused us out of bed to read the Scriptures as a family in our quiet living room. We would say morning prayers and sing songs like *All Things Bright and Beautiful* and *The Golden Morning is Fast Approaching, Jesus Soon Will Come.* Every Saturday, Mama led us on the half-mile walk to our church, York Town Seventh-day Adventist Church. Then it was home for a hot lunch. Before every meal, we thanked the Lord for His many blessings and His good graces. And we went back to church in the evenings. More than going to church, we were taught to trust in God, have faith in Him, and pray always. I accepted Jesus Christ as my Lord and Savior and was baptized at eleven years old.

Another major component of our faith was, my parents teaching us religious holidays didn't require material possessions. Those days were strictly affairs of the spirit. We were taught how to celebrate events in the Lord's life. It did not matter if we could not afford a decked-out Christmas tree or tinsel and multi-colored lights throughout the house. I remember going to Grand Market the night before Christmas. Decked out in our most beautiful clothes, we stared with wide-eyed wonder at the gifts, toys, and endless goodies. Hundreds of vendors lined up along the blocked-off, crowded streets. Papa knew his children spent the entire year counting the days until this special night. Even though he didn't have a lot of money to spare, he would always put a few coins in our hands and tell us to pick out a small gift.

My parents were two people trying to raise eleven children on a taxi driver's salary. It was hard for them to buy presents for each of us, but we did join in the gift exchange at church. Every Christmas, we looked forward to the tasty cakes my sister, Jean, would bake. At Easter, we didn't have elaborate baskets stuffed with rich chocolates and toys, but Mama made sure we enjoyed the traditional Jamaican meal of bun and cheese. My parents did their very best to make sure our holidays were unique and meaningful.

CHURCH WAS MAMA'S HOME AWAY FROM HOME. SHE TAUGHT Sabbath School, served as Deaconess, and worked for the Dorcas Society (Community Services Department). Her faith was evident in all facets of life. For example, when running her small grocery store in front of our home. She intended to sell rice, flour, sugar, and other pantry staples; but her heart was so big, she gave more than she sold. To her, it was no different than feeding the hungry children who regularly showed up at our door, which she did more times than I could count.

Almost every minute of Mama's day was spent serving others. She not only cared for my dad and ten siblings, but she also looked after her elderly mother during her illness and other children in the community. My grandmother lived with us until the day she died in our home. I was just three or four years old at the time, but I remember Mama going into her mother's room every day. She would clean her, feed her, and do everything else she could no longer do for herself. Watching Mama's compassion for others played an integral role in shaping the woman I am today.

Papa's stern face would startle some. But once they got to know him, they were amazed at his kind spirit. If you spent a few hours in his company, you would see he was an honest man. He wasn't mean, underhanded, or disrespectful. He always thanked God for His blessings. His rules for us were rigid: we had to be in bed by eight o'clock every night. But we understood his purpose was to fortify us with good judgment and respect for authority.

Although Papa laid down the law in our family and had no anxiety about enforcing it, he was gentle and loving, too. His strictness earned him the name *immigration officer* by my brothers. We had a daily ritual at our home every afternoon when Papa's taxi pulled into the driveway. My siblings and I would rush to jump in the car, scrambling to gather the coins he had purposely tossed inside.

Papa's strictness came in part from an unforgiving childhood. He'd left school before graduation to work as a tractor operator. He worked hard and was respected by his supervisors. Unfortunately, this meant he was envied by his coworkers. Some even resented that Papa's boss allowed him to be the first employee to drive any new truck. He was afforded such opportunities because of his work ethic. One day, one of those coworkers attacked Papa with a pipe, breaking his jaw. Seemingly, that coworker's feelings of envy left my father's face disfigured for life, but not his heart.

AT HOME

Our house didn't have a bathroom inside for many years until Papa built one. It was important for him that our family had one since the children were growing older. Yes, no more walking outside with a candle to the shower and outhouse at night!

Our kitchen was so small, most of our appliances were also outside until Papa built a kitchen in the house years later. Our sparse living room had a couch, a chair, and one table in the middle. In the corner was a cabinet with shelves where Mama put pictures of us growing up.

Our daily routine was simple. Papa worked five, sometimes six days a week. My siblings and I went to school Monday through Friday; Saturday was our Sabbath. Friday sunset to Saturday sunset was spent in worship. We read the Bible, memorized Scriptures, listened to sermons, and sang songs. We were taught to keep the Sabbath holy and refrain from all work. Mama reminded us, "This is the day that the Lord has made, let us rejoice and be glad in it." This is the day the Lord has blessed and sanctified.

Sunday was our prep day. We all got busy cleaning our school uniforms for the week, a prolonged activity for two reasons. First, Mama didn't have a washing machine. Second, Mama insisted everyone be involved in laundry day – her, all of us, and a helper she hired – shuffled between five different pails of water. One was for soaking, another for the first wash, another for the second wash, and separate pails for white clothes. The process was done outside on a concrete patch. She made sure the helper soaked each garment in the right pail and used the lather board, especially *on Papa's work clothes*. The dripping wet clothes were then hung to dry outside before being ironed the next day.

Every single day, Mama swept, mopped, and dusted the house. When she was done, she started on the hot meals, which had to feed thirteen mouths. Every Friday, she rode the bus for ten miles, to the May Pen Market for groceries – yams, bananas, cassava, pumpkin – which were not sold in the local stores. During the week we ate mostly vegetables. But on Sundays, what a treat! There would be chicken, beef, or even curried goat. As often as our different schedules allowed, the family sat down together around one large table.

The occasional breaks in this routine came when there was a social gathering at church. I especially enjoyed harvest time, when Mama baked pudding and other treats. After a spirit-filled service of songs, poems, and skits, we set up a beautiful display on the side of the building where we sold all the items. It was a joy to see everyone lined up to purchase a slice of Mama's pudding. They would only buy the other members' pudding after Mama's was sold out. Mama made magic in the kitchen!

I was always proud of my parents. Their respect for each other was at the center of our home. My siblings and I felt safe. We felt loved. When people ask me how I developed a can-do attitude, or how I developed character traits to sustain me through life's significant challenges, I credit my parents. They taught us the virtues leading to good character and a fulfilling life. "Tell the truth. Show compassion for those who have less. Give to the poor. Make God the center of your world." These were their lessons. How could I fail? Today, people know me as Dr. Donna Barrett, a business owner with a collection of professional licenses and certifications, not knowing my humble beginnings. I will never forget those times. I lived with my family in a modest home in a neighborhood where people looked out for each other's children.

HUMBLE BEGINNINGS, RICH LIFE

I had one baby doll growing up. Gifted from a friend when I was six years old. Oh, how I cherished my doll! Smoothing her long, black hair. Changing her scrap clothes. I loved to play outside with my friends, especially Valerie. Sometimes we were in our backyard. It was a beautiful yard with trees bearing mango, breadfruit, and ackee fruit. Other times we picked guineps, tamarind, and plums in a neighbor's yard.

I also played other games with church friends like, *Hopscotch, Go Down Immanuel Road, 1 and 20, Dandy Shandy, Hide and Seek,* and *Simon Says.* I also enjoyed going to the Denbigh show. Visiting family in Manchester, Race Course, and Kingston. Shopping in May Pen. Going to sports day at the ball-ground in York Town. Some of my favorites places to visit were Hope Garden, Green Grotto Caves, Dunn's River Falls, and Milk River Bath.

Summers were also memorable! We got to visit Mama's sister, Auntie Margaret, whom I adored. Every time I asked to go to her house, several of my siblings would beg to go too. The next thing I knew, a bunch of us were stuffing clothes into our suitcases and piling into Papa's taxi. Over the next several weeks, we were entertained by our aunt, who delighted us with stories about the love of Jesus. She baked us scrumptious puddings, picked fruit from the trees in her backyard, and told us wonderful stories about her life. On the occasions she visited our house, she would have our backs if one of us was in trouble – pleading with our parents not to spank us.

The tough part was communicating with the outside world. We mostly mailed letters. Urgent messages had to go by telegraph. Our family didn't have a phone and neither did our neighbors. On the rare occasion we needed to make a phone call, we traveled to May Pen to find a payphone. We would wait in a long line, then dial into the mainline. Each person would take their turn speaking.

I ATTENDED YORK TOWN PRIMARY, WHICH WAS ABOUT ONE mile from our home. To get there, we walked. Like church, we prayed and read Scripture in school. The teachers were strict, and the principal unforgiving. We would hurry to be on time to avoid being locked out by the principal, Miss Christie, and not miss morning devotion. Miss Christie was a real disciplinarian who carried a cane at all times. No one wanted to be sent to Miss Christie's office!

My favorite teacher, Miss Burke, was a very kind lady who lived on campus. She was attentive and noticed when students were sick. If you were distracted, she encouraged you to work harder. Miss Burke even played a large role in my acceptance into Clarendon College (*local High School*).

A noteworthy individual who impacted my life as a child was Pastor Cornelius Gray. Under his leadership, I was appointed church youth director and he encouraged me on my academic journey. I can still hear him say, "I know you will excel at Northern Caribbean University (NCU). I'd love to get you into that college." When a country girl like me wouldn't dare dream of attending such a prestigious high school as NCU, he pushed me to *believe* for more.

CLARENDON COLLEGE IT IS!

To get to school, I had to leave my house at six-thirty in the morning and catch a bus to May Pen, and sometimes another bus to Chapelton. I woke up early and got dressed in my blue and white uniform. I did not waste a minute to grab breakfast as I rushed to the bus. Mama ran behind me with a cup of hot chocolate tea and a piece of *fry dumpling* saying, "You must drink a hot cup of tea, you must line your stomach, or you will drop-down at school!"

During my studies, I favored biographies of people who overcame intense obstacles. I continued to be a good student just as in primary school. I did not rebel or harbor anger or resentment toward Mama and Papa. I did not adopt non-conformist ways. I remained on a straight path. I went to high school football games, enjoyed school trips, and hanging with my siblings. I loved listening to Bob Marley's reggae music and reading books and magazines. As most teenage girls, I was interested in boys, but I always heard the voice of my parents in the back of my mind saying, "Don't mess around with boys. Stay focused on your schoolwork!" My parent's teachings allowed me to form the thoughts, *whatever the mind can conceive, it can achieve. No matter the circumstances or challenges.*

ME? SUSPENDED?

I was thirteen, sitting in Spanish class and bored out of my brains.

I noticed a driver ready to hop into a car outside my window. I waved him down and thankfully, he was going to May Pen! Those rides were hard to come by and it could take hours to get home by bus. We had three minutes until dismissal.

Without further thought, I and two classmates jumped in the car with the entire class watching. Pretty soon, everyone had filed out the classroom to observe our spectacle. The teacher motioned for the driver to stop and told us to exit the vehicle. After the bell rang, he sent us to the principal's office. Instead, we all went home.

The next day a note indicated I was still to report to the principal's office, and I still did not go. Neither did the other students. The principal came looking for us and we were suspended on the spot! Reentry to class required a meeting with our parents.

Now, I was in a bind! Telling either of my parents was out of the question. I racked my brain but came up with only one solution. Act like nothing had happened and hope for the best. Typical teenager scared out of her wits. For the next few days, I dressed for school each morning and left the house as if I were catching the bus.

Mama didn't suspect a thing.

I took the bus to Chapelton. May Pen was filled with people who knew I should have been in school. Then, I spent the entire day walking the streets until it was time to catch a bus home. I pulled it off, although I was not as successful in coping with the guilt I felt inside. This was out of character for the young lady I was raised to be. Even worse, I still had not solved the major problem: how would I get back into school? Thankfully my sister, Yvonne, was visiting, and she came to my rescue. I vowed never again to put myself in such a dicey situation. Mama did not find out until decades later.

COTS ON DIRT FLOORS

During the summer following my third year, I was hired for a temporary government job. I was required to visit impoverished communities in May Pen. I tracked and reported their needs. I will never forget the hardship I witnessed there. Jamaica has never been a rich country. Unemployment is rampant. I was aware of the economic impact, but until the summer job, I had no idea just how dehumanizing poverty was.

I saw people living in temporary shacks. I saw people sleeping on cots on dirt floors. Many did not have food or money to buy school supplies for their children. No one in the district even hoped to have what I had grown accustomed to – a father with steady wages, a roof over my head, good food on the table, clothes on my back, or a house with a solid foundation. Let alone a refrigerator or television. I started to understand how fortunate I was. I thanked God for everything He provided to my family. I vowed never to forget His blessings. Most of all, I thanked Him for opening my eyes. I had taken the job only to earn money, yet I ended up receiving so much more! Once the job ended, I went back to school in the fall to complete my studies and earned my high school diploma.

I often thought of those unfortunate people I encountered on that summer job, yet I had no idea how to help. As a sixteen-year-old with no money of my own, what could I do? This job was, in many ways, a turning point for me. I knew if I ever had the opportunity to help those in need, I would take it. I would serve God's children. No matter the circumstances, I would find a way.

LIKE EVERY OTHER LITTLE GIRL, I OFTEN IMAGINED LIFE AS AN adult. When friends asked me what I wanted to be when I grew up, I didn't have to think for a second.

"A teacher!" I said proudly, most of the time. Then, other times, I would say I wanted to own a car, live in an *upstairs house*, and run my own business. These things were out of reach for my family and most of our neighbors. Some of them resorted to farming, cleaning the streets, or taking day jobs in construction because they couldn't find steady work. I knew people in Jamaica had few opportunities. I knew many of my classmates would not find jobs after high school. They would eventually give up even trying. Like my parents, many would sacrifice education and take whatever work came their way just to feed their families.

Mama and Papa never wanted the same life for their kids. They raised us to believe the future is bright for those engaged in honest pursuits and who followed the Lord's teachings. I never stopped wanting the things I dreamt of as a child. They might be out of reach for most Jamaicans, but I knew they were common for people in other countries. I learned this from listening to stories of family and friends who had left Jamaica for colder climates but more prosperous economies. I also knew if I wanted them badly enough, I would have to make sacrifices.

Above all, I would have to *believe*.

"YOU CAN'T STAY IN JAMAICA!" MAMA SAID. "I WANT THE BEST for you. I don't want you to lose your focus."

I graduated high school the week before. But having a diploma didn't equal a job in Jamaica. It could be weeks or months before I could find a good one. This worried Mama. Those were the weeks and months when single new graduates created lives they would not want in the long run. To Mama, free time meant trouble. She had a plan and worked fast to set it in motion.

I would have to leave my family.

The only country I had ever called home.

It was not going to be easy. But even I had to admit; it was the only way.

Now that you've experienced the view from the Atrium, let's ascend to Deck Two for the next segment of our voyage.

Deck 2

EMBARKATION: STARTING THE VOYAGE

"Believe Hard Work Will Pay-off!"

LIKE WAVES CRASHING INTO THE SIDE OF THE SHIP, HERE I was. Swaying back and forth. Back and forth. Between the life I knew and the life I dreamed of knowing. Feeling like it was time to gain control.

It was time to trust the Captain, who guided my life's direction. Embarking on a new voyage would be no easy task. There would be a rocky journey ahead of me. But I was ready. Ready to embrace the next phase of my womanhood, which required me to let go of my inhibitions.

If I was going to make my family proud and accomplish the plan the Captain laid out for me, I had to leap. The time to set sail was now.

THE NORMAN MANLEY INTERNATIONAL AIRPORT IN
Kingston was abuzz on June 10, 1979. The sapphire-blue sky was
soft and bright. The Jamaican sun was blistering. Mom and a few of
my siblings came to see me off. There were tears. Hugs. Beautiful
parting words.

"God will be with you always!"

Mama being Mama, the usual warnings, "Do not give your
sister any trouble!"

The day was not about endings. It was about a new beginning.

I was on my way to the Bahamas, a trip conceived in Mama's
mind months before school ended. She meant what she said. I was
not staying in Jamaica. Within days of my graduation, Mama called
Yvonne in Nassau to make the arrangements.

"Yes, of course, Donna can stay with me," Yvonne said as she
promptly sent the ticket.

I would be staying with Yvonne, who lived in Nassau ever since
graduating from high school and landing a job with Air Jamaica.
She was married and had become a legal resident. Yvonne had
broken out of the cycle of no opportunities in Jamaica. Mama knew
I could do the same.

Yvonne lived in a welcoming, middle-class neighborhood. She
had a lovely house with a separate bedroom just for me. The
Bahamas was supposed to be the place where I would make my first
real strides toward a career. But life seemed to have other plans.

I remember it as a time for my coming of age. I enjoyed getting
to know Yvonne's friends; they were good people. I spent twelve
blissful months acclimating myself to the mild climate, luxurious
beaches, food festivals, the people, and cultural entertainment
activities of the Bahamas. I did not have to worry about finding a
job. Yvonne supported me. I devoted all my energy toward
applying for college. I wanted to be a teacher or maybe an accoun-
tant. Even a job in business sounded good. Surely the country had a
decent number of colleges and programs to prepare me for any of
those careers.

And it did.

But there was an issue.

I had no access to them. I found each program of my interest required proof of legal residence. I also knew I would not be able to get any proof anytime soon. I had a six-month period of which I could remain in the Bahamas legally; Then, I applied for a six-month extension. After it expired, I had to go back to Jamaica to re-apply.

After Yvonne helped me return to Jamaica, instead of going home to York Town. I opted to stay with a friend in Old Harbor. If I returned home, I would have walked into a line of questions I was not prepared to answer. Do you have a job? Are you in school? Why are you back so soon?

I planned to make my return to Jamaica a short visit. I came back on a mission to apply for a visa to the United States. America was my golden ticket. An even bigger prize than going back to the Bahamas. I submitted my application at the American embassy in Kingston. DENIED. The immigration officer looked me up and down.

> *"You're not going to come back here," he announced.*
> *Before I could ask how he came to this conclusion,*
>   *he went on to explain.*
> *"You don't have any ties to Jamaica," he said. "You*
>   *don't own a home or a business. You don't even*
>   *have a job."*

He was right, I had none of those things. But what I did have was a spirit even his dour expression couldn't dampen. I believed in my abilities. One opportunity can open a whole door of possibilities.

I marched out the embassy without a visa, but with determination. I couldn't go to the United States yet, but I got busy making arrangements to return to the Bahamas. Before I knew it, I was in the Nassau airport again! After deplaning, I was questioned on why I had returned so quickly. Thankfully, I knew what to say! My answers were good enough to guarantee another six months on the island. This solved a big problem, but this leg of the journey wasn't over. I still faced another roadblock: establishing residency. Sure, I had made it back to the Bahamas, but I was still *illegal*. If I wanted to stay, I would have to *hide*. The question became, how long could I remain hidden?

THE ANNOUNCEMENT CAME A FEW WEEKS AFTER I ARRIVED IN the Bahamas.

Immigration officers would be raiding homes for illegal aliens! I was home one day when I heard a knock on the door. Yvonne and her husband had gone out to run some errands. It was just me and my baby nephew, Dave, inside. I peeped through the window and could not believe my eyes. A government van was parked out front. Immigration officers were walking through the yard. I grabbed my nephew and led him into the closet and told him to stay put. Then I hid under the bed, listening as the officers walked the perimeter of the house.

I started to sweat.

It was so hard to stay calm. All I could do was pray the officers would leave, and Yvonne would return soon. My nephew began to hum, and I gestured for him to be quiet. He didn't stop. I crawled from under the bed, made it to the closet, and placed my hand over his mouth, hugging him tightly.

"Don't worry, everything will be alright," I whispered.

It took thirty minutes for the knocking to stop. I still had no idea if it was safe to look, but I couldn't wait. I crawled up to a window to look outside. Finally! They were gone. Yvonne came soon after. I broke down, telling her the nightmare I had just been through. A week later, while talking to a neighbor, Yvonne learned she had been reported for harboring an illegal resident at her house.

A nerve-racking few weeks followed. I was petrified to leave the house or go anywhere without Yvonne. I was only eighteen years old! Just the thought of being picked up by immigration police and deported to Jamaica scared me. I stayed inside. But my solution was temporary. I could not live in fear and in hiding forever.

I had to find a way.

Out.

I had to escape.

IN THE MEANTIME, I LOOKED FOR A JOB. I DIDN'T HAVE A WORK permit or residency papers. I knew I had to tread lightly, and I knew it was dangerous. My first attempts went nowhere. I became more disappointed each day. Then, an opportunity fell into my lap. A nearby pharmacist gave me a cashier position. I was so relieved to have a job; I didn't even ask about pay. Compensation was just $50 for a Sunday through Friday shift.

I had a job and was making my own money. I stayed focused, kept my head down, but my guard up. With this routine, my immigration status could stay private. I could earn a living at Yvonne's and avoid deportation. At least until I could come up with a long-term plan.

Working gave me courage. I began to take leaps. Knowing it was a longshot, I was bold enough to apply to The College of the Bahamas' accounting program. DENIED. *Lack of credentials!* I, then, applied for an education program. After all, I dreamed of being a teacher as a child. DENIED. *Lack of residency proof!*

Another dead end.

As time went on, the rejections weighed heavily on me. I could not shake the overwhelming disappointment I felt. Or the powerlessness. It was as though I had stumbled into a ditch and no idea of how to pull myself out.

If I were someone else, I may have thought I had to do this on my own. But I knew better. Because of Mama, I knew God is the vine, and we are the branches. Without Him, we can do *nothing* (John 15:5). Recalling Scripture, I lifted my eyes to the Savior. I prayed for an answer. And I had no doubt God heard me. He saw my plight.

I was not going to give up because help was on the way.

My Boarding Currency

A friend invited me to join an ASUE (*savings club*). My contribution would be $40 a week, which was a challenge because I was still earning just $50 a week. I accepted the challenge and my savings grew.

$1,500 would get me to America!

A friend invited me to a meeting at a local restaurant. It was the opportunity I'd been in search of but packaged much differently than I expected. The details were simple. Fifteen hundred dollars would land me a spot on a ship to the United States and thanks to the ASUE, I had the money. We were not to bring anything with us, except the clothes on our backs. I had to admit it sounded sketchy. So many things could go wrong! And who was I getting involved with anyway? Who were the people in charge of this trip? What would stop them from running off with my money? I spent the next two weeks in agony.

Should I take the risk?

Should I follow my dreams? In an unconventional way?

Is it worth it?

I went over the pros and cons. I always came to the same conclusion. It was risky! BUT it might be the *only* way to America. It was this thought my mind meditated on. *Over and over.* This thought wrestled with the knowledge of God watching over me. Then, I came to my senses and made up my mind:

Yes, I would board the ship! I would give it a shot.

But Yvonne wanted no part of it, and she was skeptical.

"What if something happens to you?" she asked. "What in the world would I tell Mama and Papa?"

I did not have an answer for her, but I was not deterred. I believed in the power of God. I believed He would protect me. I believed His words, "I will never leave you nor forsake you" (Hebrews 13:5b). I believed, deep in my heart, God had a plan for me. He was paving my road with obstacles intended to strengthen, rather than defeat me.

I understood Yvonne's doubts. They were born out of concern and love for me, her younger sister. I knew she felt responsible for me. She would have to answer to Mama if anything happened to me. I understood my safety was her utmost concern. Yet, as strange as this may sound, my desire to go felt less like *personal* ambition and more like a *calling*.

It felt much more like a willingness to accept the Will of God. After all, God inspired Mama to get me out of Jamaica. Right? Had the Lord not also thwarted my efforts to advance in the Bahamas? Best of all, was it not the Lord who positioned me on this path? It certainly felt to me I was accepting the Lord's plan. If it meant enduring risks, so be it.

I was willing. I trusted His guidance.

The more I thought about it, the more I saw I did not have much of a choice. Living in the Bahamas meant living in fear, accepting I couldn't continue my education, and perhaps could not rise above a cashier's job. Those facts were undeniable. They made the trip to America much more worthy. America was a country of endless opportunities. People all over knew this to be true. For proof, I needed to look no further than my brother, Robert. He'd been living in the United States since leaving Jamaica in the seventies. He had a wife and his own home. He made good money as a mechanic for tractor-trailers.

WE MET AT A RESTAURANT CLOSE TO WHERE THE SHIPS SET sail. I arrived by van earlier in the evening. Parting with Yvonne was still fresh in my mind. "What did you expect?" she said many years later. "You had just come to live in the Bahamas, and without staying too long, you wanted to go to America *without papers!*" I boarded the ship wearing blue jeans, a red and white blouse, and sneakers. I held nothing, but $200 in my pocket, enough to start my new life. No doubt about it now.

I was headed to America!

I REMEMBER THE FEAR I FELT WHEN WE TRIED TO EXIT THE ship. As if it were yesterday. The crewmen surrounded us, demanding identification. We might have been mere moments away from police custody. The situation had come to a chilly standstill until, by some miracle, another crewman stepped forward. A man none of us knew.

He addressed his crew members.

"These are my friends," he said, nodding in our direction. "They always visit me. You can let them go."

YOU CAN LET THEM GO.

WHAT A SHOCK TO HEAR THOSE WORDS FROM THE MOUTH OF A complete stranger; a good soul who saw us in trouble and jumped in to vouch for us at precisely the right time. It felt as though a cinder block had been removed from my chest. The crewmen who had surrounded us began to step back.

How hard it was not to embrace this man. This angel of God! How hard it was to hold back the tears and expressions of joy. But I had to keep up the pretense. Next, I lunged down the ship's stairs, too scared to look back!

Feeling on top of the world, feeling free as a bird. I made it! I was here.

Run, run, RUN.

I sprinted towards a taxi parked near the port in downtown Miami. Florida's climate lived up to its reputation. The breezeless air was hot and moist. I jumped in the taxi with two of my ship-mates. We drove until I remembered I had no money to pay. Neither did the other passengers. I needed to reach Robert, who lived about 15 miles away.

I spotted a payphone and asked the driver to stop at a nearby supermarket. Robert was at work, but he had a general idea of when the ship would arrive. Yvonne had called him after she and I said goodbye. (Much later, I found out Yvonne called Robert every ten minutes following my departure.)

What a relief when I saw Robert's wife, Maize, driving into the supermarket parking lot. Maize paid the driver, and we took off. But even as the car pushed through Miami Gardens, miles away from the port, I still did not feel completely safe. I spent the whole ride feeling paranoid. Making sure no one was following us.

When we finally made it to Robert's home, the bathroom was my first destination. My bladder was about to burst! Second, I had to call my family in Jamaica to make them aware of my new country of residence. I had no idea how they'd handle the news.

"Hi, Mama," I said, "I've made it! I'm in the United States."

Better to get it all out at once, I reasoned. Although remembering the call makes me chuckle now. Those words must have delivered an electric shock to Mama's brain. *"What??!!"* "Yes, Mama. I'm at brother Robert's." "But *how* did you get there?" she asked. The question was to be expected, although it's the one I most dreaded. I didn't answer, as I saw no reason to worry her with the details at that point.

I HAD BEEN AT ROBERT'S HOME JUST A FEW DAYS WHEN THE ship which brought me to America made the evening news. There it was. On TV! The same ship was returning to the same dock, the Port of Miami.

But with one crucial difference.

The latest bunch of contraband passengers had been outed. The men who were in charge of us had been captured. All were arrested and were now being deported.

Oh my. God is amazing!

He is always present in times of trouble! I shook my head. Here I am, cozy in Robert's living room. The horror of the trip behind me. This news report was a reminder the situation for me could have ended quite differently. Instead of being sprawled out on his couch, I could have been wearing handcuffs. Sharing the backseat of a police car. Headed to jail. The proof was on the screen in front of me. If I had ever wanted assurance a guardian angel was watching over me, I had it now.

NEW TO AMERICA AND PLANNING MY NEXT MOVE. ROBERT

had opened his home to me without conditions. But I was never one to depend on others. I wanted money and possessions of my own. But I had entered the country without going through the proper channels. Even now, American employers shy away from undocumented workers.

Answering phones, ringing up customers. You name it. I was willing to do it.

I began looking for a job at once, mostly in the hefty career section of the Sunday newspaper. I focused on entry-level jobs, not requiring a college degree. The language would not be an issue. I grew up speaking Jamaican Patois, an English variation. But thanks to my teachers back home, I spoke English well enough to communicate in America.

I was beyond excited! I found an employer willing to provide on-the-job training for a secretarial job. But I was disappointed when they told me to bring my social security card with me. Oh well, there were many more jobs to choose from. The next posting was for a cashier's position near Robert's home. The $4.50/hour wages the manager offered sounded great to me. Finally, I had hit the jackpot!

The supervisor was a pleasant woman in her fifties. I could tell she liked me. She encouraged me to learn the job well so I could be promoted in the future. She even helped me through the social security situation.

"How in the world could you have made such a mistake?" she asked when it was discovered my paycheck had the wrong social security number.

What I didn't tell – *couldn't* tell her – I was to blame for the mistake. The number I had put on my job application was false. The real number came in the mail weeks later, when I had finally been issued a valid social security card. The problem then was to figure out a way to tell my employer. I feigned ignorance, but her initial reaction made me worry. Was she on to my deception? I'm not sure. But she accompanied me to the human resources department and helped me explain the mishap.

Another dangerously close call.

I GOT MY PAYCHECK AFTER ONE WEEK. ONE HUNDRED DOLLARS was mine to spend on whatever I wanted. I bought new clothes and some toiletries, and I was thrilled because I did not need to ask my brother for one cent.

I loved the job – the friendly coworkers, my encouraging supervisor. I thought of staying a long time, maybe even becoming a supervisor! I loved my beautiful new surroundings. The big homes, big cars, beautiful highways stretching in every direction. Every detail of public life in America seemed to be so perfectly planned. Quite different from Jamaica or the Bahamas.

I overlooked the annoyance of not being a legal resident. I did not mind keeping a low profile until I could get papers. This was the country for people like me who wanted an *upstairs house* and a business with my name on it! The legal residence would come in time. I didn't question settling in America.

I felt I was where I belonged.

I was at home. In my new country.

I finally began to feel peace as the waves of life began to steady. No more swaying. I was ready for this leg of the journey. What else would my Captain have in store for me?

Deck 3

DOUBLE OCCUPANCY: A NEW JOURNEY

"*When you face tough times, Believe there is light at the end of the tunnel and stay the course.*"

New passengers have come aboard. More love and laughter fill the air on the ship.

This journey, taken away from those who raised me, has not been comfortable. This journey, taken away from those who knew me best, has not been easy. But our latest additions to the ship are keeping the trip lively! The joy is growing. The warmth is growing. The family is growing.

Thank you, Captain, for keeping me surrounded while I cruise along these rocky waters!

I remember when we first laid eyes on each other. He was cool. Calm. As handsome as could be. His eyes were mesmerizing. They could tell many stories by themselves. With butterflies in my stomach, I often looked away when I caught his gaze. What an effect he had on me.

We met on Thanksgiving in 1982. It was my first American holiday! The house was filled with the laughter of friends and family. Robert introduced me to one of his guests named Philip. *Philip.* There was an instant spark between us. I only hesitated when he asked for my number. I didn't own a phone. I gave him Robert's number, hoping my brother would understand. I could not miss the opportunity to get to know the man who caught my eye.

During our first conversation, I learned many exciting things about Philip. He had recently completed a four-year stint as a Marine. He went on to work for a local news station before landing a job with the United States Post Office. Philip was new to North Miami, although his mother lived around the block from Robert. His parents – Dad from Jamaica, Mom from Montserrat – had migrated to England years earlier. They later moved to New York after Philip was born.

I shared my life story with him also. We talked for hours. It was as if we'd known each other for years. When we said our goodbyes, I anxiously waited to hear his voice again. The next morning, he called and offered me a ride to work. Of course, I couldn't turn him down! This ride was the first of many. It felt nice to trade my bus rides for a chance to get to know this compelling man. I was falling fast.

AS OUR LOVE GREW, SO DID OUR LIFE AS A COUPLE. PHILIP AND I moved in together in February 1983. We settled in his new one-bedroom apartment in Miami Gardens, about five or six miles from Robert's home. Every time I pass by it today, I remember how liberating it felt to finally have a place of my own.

A few months later, our family grew bigger. Our daughter, Kameisha, was born December 6, 1983. My precious first-born, such a cute little thing! Leaving her to return to work was no easy task. A sitter helped out for a few weeks, but I couldn't stand being without her during the day. So, I quit my job to put every ounce of my energy into being a mother. I wanted to raise my daughter as lovingly as Mama raised us. Above all, I wanted to teach Kameisha to love the Lord and accept His ultimate power in her heart.

My dreams were continuing to unfold before my eyes. A loving relationship. A warm and cozy home. A beautiful baby girl. Philip and I seemed to have it all. But there was still something missing.

A ring.

I desired marriage, but it seemed to be the furthest thing from Philip's mind. Would he ever propose? How could I get him to walk down the aisle? I decided to take matters into my own hands. "I've decided on a wedding date," I said one day, having no clue how he'd respond. Philip didn't seem to be surprised. He simply said, "Okay, just tell me where and when, and I'll be there." His response held all the enthusiasm of a husband who had been told to pick up the dry cleaning. To this day, we laugh about this moment!

The big day had come. December 22, 1984. It was a cool and windy day. I woke up ecstatic to see our beautiful church, glorious cake, and the vast reception hall. I arrived at my friend Marcia's house early, my nerves soothed by a steaming cup of tea her mother had just poured. My sister and maid of honor, Jean, helped me with my hair and make-up. Once I put on my radiant white gown, I was ready to make my way to the altar.

Our family and friends had gathered to celebrate our nuptials. Philip's entire family came; however, Mama and Papa didn't have enough time to secure paperwork to enter the United States legally. The wedding date had been set pretty quickly. But I did have all my siblings and lots of friends attend. With a wedding party of twelve, Philip and I felt loved and supported the entire day.

My blue and white-flowered bouquet beamed as I held onto Robert's arm down the aisle. Lionel Richie's *My Love* softly played as guests smiled at me. I will never forget the nerves sweeping over me as I approached the altar. I wondered if my guests could tell my stomach was fluttering as I gazed upon my handsome groom. Philip stood there with a smile as calm as the sea. A smile that soon began to make me feel at ease.

I can do this. Lord, be with me.

We exchanged sweet vows. I thanked the Lord for choosing Philip as my husband. With him by my side, I knew I could conquer whatever the world threw my way. Thirty-five years later, we're still together. Still madly in love!

Philip and I were newlyweds, seeking a bigger space to call home. Just before the lease ended on our apartment, we closed the deal on a foreclosed property. It needed a lot of work. At the time, Philip was twenty-three, and I was twenty-one. It wasn't common for people our age to be homeowners. They were either leaving home for the first time or graduating from college.

But we felt ready. Philip learned the ins and outs of real estate from his father, who made good money buying properties and renting them out. And even though I was up to my ears in baby laundry, I was wide-eyed thinking about the new challenge. My brother Kenneth thought "Are you out of your mind?" when he got his first look at our new place. He had a point. This was a big project. But I've always been someone who could see smooth surfaces where others only saw bumps. I believe in my abilities, and I know I can accomplish anything I set my mind to.

One step at a time, Donna.

I repeated this to myself as I surveyed the house from top to bottom. I started writing a master list of problem areas. After Philip and I packed every item we owned into one small room, we got to work. New ceilings. New cabinets. New countertops. Shiny appliances in the kitchen. Fresh tile and fixtures in the bathrooms. Sturdy walls and floors throughout. And not to forget, a new nursery for our beautiful baby girl! Room by room, we knocked down and built up again. My brother later visited for another look. He couldn't believe the progress we made! The fixer-upper priced at $47,500 in 1983 went for twice that amount when we sold it fifteen years later. *Success!*

To us, this project meant much more than a profit. It taught us what could be accomplished with intuition and teamwork. Then, it hit me. Real estate! I was interested in *real estate*. Turning a small deposit into an investment we were proud to live in was a huge turning point for me. My duties as wife and mother came first, but the new flame lit within me continued to burn. My career life was about to change.

I PUT OFF MAKING A CAREER-CHANGING DECISION UNTIL MY supervisor from my previous job called. "I can't hold your job any longer," she said. So, I reached for the low-hanging fruit and went back to my former position. For the next few weeks, I tried to focus on working while getting used to the idea of Kameisha in daycare. But still, I couldn't do it. So, once again, I quit the job and became a full-time stay-at-home mom.

But then, there was my older brother, Kenneth, who had a proposal. It was hard to turn down. "But I have a baby to care for!" I told Kenneth, who asked me to run his new companies, a gas station, and a trucking business. "That's no problem," Kenneth said. "Take her with you!" Although we needed a second paycheck, I didn't want to leave my precious baby in someone else's care. Yes, being able to care for Kameisha while at work would solve the dilemma I faced since she was born. But I still had doubts. Should I go back to work or raise my baby full-time?

I could collect a paycheck and care for Kameisha *full-time*. And Robert was willing to work nights and weekends to help with the trucking business. My other brother, Tony, would also be one of the drivers and would help to care for the trucks. But there was another, even bigger problem: this was a business I had no experience with. But Kenneth still trusted me to run it. "You can do it," said my brother, a successful businessman since coming to Miami Gardens in the early eighties. "Well, if you think I can, I'm willing to try," I replied.

And I did.

One day at a time. I learned about my role. Before I knew it, I mastered keeping books and managing day-to-day tasks such as working with gasoline vendors. I was in charge of making almost every decision for the company's daily functioning—a big job for someone with no experience. But Kenneth believed in me. And I believed in myself. By now, it's clear: I don't back down from challenges.

Unfortunately, this experience came to a close when Kenneth returned to Jamaica and closed the business. However, I still appreciated the chance to prove myself. I had what it took to manage a company. *Me.* I had no idea I would develop such a skill. But I knew it was just a matter of time before I used it for my advancement. Running a business was in my blood.

STARTING LIFE IN A NEW COUNTRY. ENTERING THE workforce. Motherhood. Marriage. What was the next challenge I could conquer? My educational pursuit. Could a small-town girl from Jamaica earn a degree from an American college? As a busy stay-at-home mom, I had no time to figure this out. But Philip believed I could do it. In January 1986, he told me to hop in our car for a surprise excursion. Where on earth could we be headed?

Miami Dade Community College (MDCC). He pulled up to the front of the school. It was his way of showing his support for my educational desires. I'm not sure how he knew school was on my radar at the time. Philip just knew. He always knew what was on my heart. I remember telling him about my attempts to attend school in the Bahamas a while back. I also knew he was impressed with my ability to shift Kenneth's start-up into a profitable venture. "You're ready for this challenge," he said. Although I was a self-confident woman, hearing those words from the man I loved gave me the strength to move forward.

There was one more hurdle to conquer. Before I could apply for an American college, I needed a GED. My Jamaican high school diploma was not enough. So, I did what had to be done. GED classes were held nightly, from six to nine every Monday through Thursday. I signed up for the courses and even had a study partner—my nephew, Antonio, who dropped out of high school. Together, we tackled our GED program.

After completing my program, I moved on to taking Business Administration classes at MDCC. All while caring for our newest family member – my second baby girl, Nekeisha. She entered the world on July 15, 1986. Another *beautiful* addition to our lives. Philip didn't want motherhood and work to interfere with my studies, so he made some sacrifices. He began to work earlier in the day. I was able to attend class and study while he cared for the girls. We made our new schedule work until I received my Associate of Arts degree in June 1987.

I could not have done this without his support. He wanted me to have a college degree. Not to improve our family income, but for me to fulfill one of my life's goals. We were already making good money. So, Philip simply wanted to see me accomplish what I yearned to do since leaving Jamaica. My mother-in-law and my sister, Jean, also helped. Our reliable babysitters! Philip and I were two young parents of two small girls. We needed love and support to advance in the world. I couldn't imagine life without our village.

AN UNEXPECTED PACKAGE
Mama made it to the United States!

It took five years after I arrived for her to make her first visit. I hadn't seen her since my husband and I took Kameisha to Jamaica soon after she was born. Yvonne accompanied her. I truly missed them both! Having them there made our home feel complete.

During their visit, we were planning Kameisha's third birthday. Of course, I had to bring them with me to go shopping for the occasion. We were all so excited about the party. Little did we know, the excitement we felt would be short-lived. After I pulled up to the house, Mom and Yvonne carried Kameisha and Nekeisha inside. I kept the front door slightly ajar because we had more packages to unload. As I headed back out to the car, I noticed a man. Standing at my front door. I didn't recognize him.

"Can I help you?" I said.

"Is Donna here?" he said.

I just stood there. *How did this stranger know my name?* Before I could open my mouth to answer, he jerked his head. Giving some type of signal with his hand. In the blink of an eye, four men barged into my house. All holding guns. Three of them pushed me, Mama, Yvonne, and my daughters into a bedroom. The fourth one stood by the door, watching over us.

The men began to pull out the phones from our walls. They ransacked our house, seemingly searching for money. I thought maybe they assumed money from the gas station was being held in my home. There was no other reason for a group of men to rob my family. But, of course, we didn't keep the company's money there. When they couldn't find anything, they settled for stealing any jewelry they could find. They found Yvonne's purse on the counter and emptied it. Even the earrings she wore were ripped off, splitting her ear.

Feelings of chaos and fear filled the house. *How could this be happening to us? My mother, my sister, and my daughters! All our lives were in danger!* Mama and I just sat there. Motionless. In utter shock. Wondering if they were going to shoot us. Was this the end?

Yvonne was in a panic. She started to scream, "We don't have no money!" I shushed her down. "Don't say a word," I whispered. "The best thing to do is to stay calm." It seemed like an eternity had passed before we heard a car horn honk. The group of men finally ran out. For a while, we all just continued to sit in fear. Too afraid to look out the window. Eventually, I got up the nerve to run across the street to my neighbors to phone the police! The rest of the day was a blur. I couldn't even form the words to describe the situation. I can still see the look of horror on Mama's face.

For months, I didn't feel safe in *my own home*. My heart would race if I noticed a car driving up and down the street. I had Philip lookout for me when I came home after dark. It also took Mama a while to visit again. We were all traumatized. Still, we were thankful the Lord spared our lives. He saved my family. Experiencing this led me to look at life through a different lens. Deciding to rededicate my life to Christ, I was rebaptized at the Tabernacle Seventh-day Adventist Church.

Not long after, Pastor Gray was assigned to a new church in the United States, Pem-Mar Seventh-day Adventist Church. He invited me to join, so I gladly accepted. There, I have served in leadership for many years until now. While the circumstances weren't ideal, I am thankful for the push to revive my relationship with the Lord. Becoming closer-connected to the Source and a community of believers is what I needed to continue my journey.

The waters may appear uncertain and even daunting at times, but I'm trusting the Master of the seas. Moving forward. His hands keeping my fellow passengers and me steady.

Afloat.

Phil's Birthday

Cru

*We Salute Phil for
his Service to Our Country!*

Phil after Work

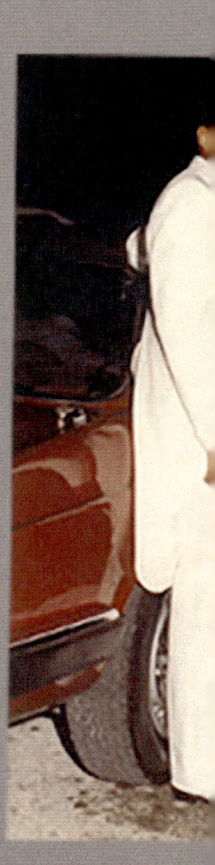

Our

Phil, Donna & Baby

Our First Home

Donna & Philip

Donna's Birthday

The Happy Couple

ng Day

Family

Donna and Daughters
(lt to rt): Chante', Nekeisha
& Kameisha

Donna and her siste[r]
Yvonne (lt) & Jean

Donna's Brothers,
Winston & Tony

Donna, Daughters &
Granddaughters

Donna's Daughters (lt to rt): Kar[...]

Donna with Kameisha
& Nekeisha

Donna's Mom & Dad

Donna's First Home

Donna and Siblings:
Kenneth,
Yvonne & Winston

Chante' & Nekeisha

Family & Friends

A Special Thanks

*Being Hoode
& Dr. Barclay*

Grad

Phil on Graduation Day

Grandma Gets Her P

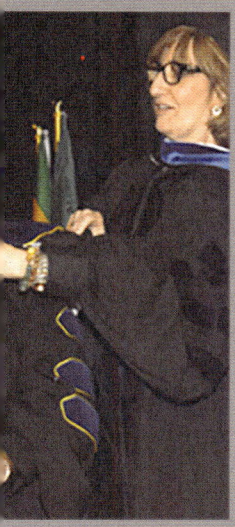

r. Benoliel

tion

My Core Supporters

Bachelor's

Master's

Donna at 17

Donna's First Job

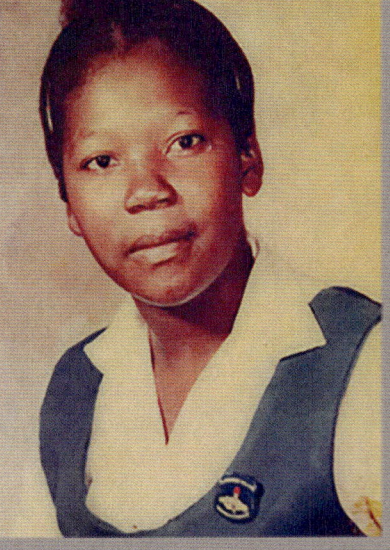

Young Donna

Donna's Graduation Party

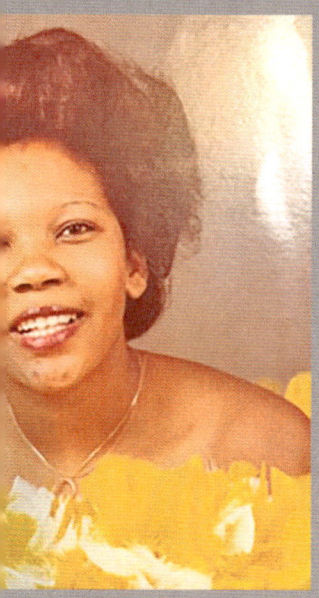

onna

The Lovely Lady

a in Bahamas

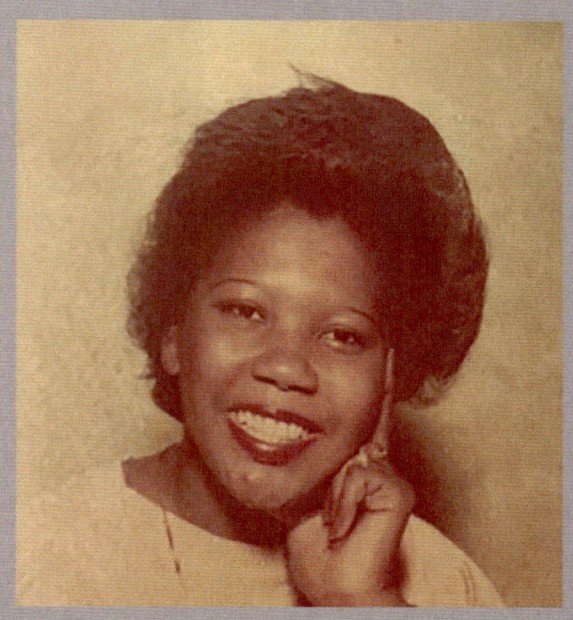

Donna at 18

Deck 4

MINI SUITE: TAKING THE CORPORATE ROUTE

"*Belief, Faith, and Trust in God are the three foundational elements that will lead you to a Life of Purpose.*"

I CAN FEEL THE SHIP BEGINNING TO TURN. PUSHING AGAINST the smooth, but strong waters. The route I once knew is shifting. But I'm ready to see where it goes. What's to come? The new adventures ahead of me. Even the challenges I may have to face along the way. I'm ready for it all.

I've given the Captain control. I'm just sailing along His route.

BEING WITHOUT A JOB AFTER THE CLOSING OF KENNETH'S business didn't worry me much. I found joy in raising my two baby girls. But I sought employment once our finances got a little tight. This would be my first post-grad job search! I could now add an associate degree to my resume. Opportunities that were once unavailable were now fair game. It was my time to enter the corporate world.

Not long into my search, a prominent phone company called me for an interview. I was brought on as a customer service representative in Hollywood, Florida. For two years, I held the most advanced job I'd ever had. Working there gave me hope of climbing the ladder within the company. I had a position with what was then the world's largest telephone provider, so the opportunities were limitless.

Until they weren't.

At my two-year anniversary, the company announced it was closing the Florida location. Here I was, back on the market for another job. This was a huge letdown. I should have been crushed and discouraged. But I was more annoyed than anything. I finally found a job that fit my family's routine with good pay and a chance to move up. Circumstances were beyond my control. So, I tweaked my resume and kept moving forward. Ready to start my search over again.

But life took another turn.

On March 14, 1990, we welcomed our third bundle of joy. My precious daughter, Chante'! Although motherhood brought me great pleasure, I had to put my career on hold again. At least until Philip and I agreed on needing a second paycheck for the lifestyle we became accustomed to having. So, I eventually returned to the workforce. Fortunately, my stay-at-home mom days didn't hold me back from landing good-paying positions. I was offered a higher-level customer service position with another leading phone service company. Ready to jump into this new role, I was about to learn the true meaning of working in corporate America. The ups and the *downs*.

The ship may be on a different course, but I was made for the ride.

I was created for this.

I was destined to be on this journey.

I'll continue to stay aboard until my ship docks again. As the tides go in and out.

In and out.

Deck 5

INTERIOR STATEROOM: PUBLIC VS. PRIVATE
RELATIONS

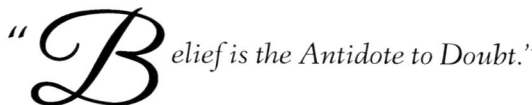

"Belief is the Antidote to Doubt."

EACH WAVE HITS THE SHIP A LITTLE HARDER. THE SEAS ARE becoming angrier as the skies turn gray. Thunder roaring as lightning zigzags against the clouds. Storms were in the forecast. But no one expected it to be this heavy. We sit quietly in our rooms, waiting for it to pass over. What's stopping us from tipping over?

We are anchored. Anchored in the Captain's power.

Nothing can stop us from cruising along.

READY TO MOVE ON TO THE NEXT PHASE IN MY CAREER, I WAS excited to learn about another great opportunity from a former coworker. The operator for the phone company I previously worked with had an opening. I wasted no time applying! Several nail-biting weeks went by. My excitement turned into anxiousness. Working for an industry giant again would be huge for me. Not only would it look great on my resume, but the job offered excellent pay and benefits for my family.

Then, I got the call. I was invited in for an interview. I did the best I could to make a great impression. It worked – I made it to the second round. Knowing what was at stake, I turned to the one I knew I could always count on. *Dear Father, be with me during the interview process. Give me the right words to say. Inspire me to give the correct answers.* As always, a warm feeling came over me. I felt at peace.

Days later, I got the call I had been waiting for. I was offered the job!

Like many positions, my new opportunity came with its set of challenges. Even before my first day, I faced my first hurdle. All candidates for that position had to pass an entire month of training, including two weeks out of state in Atlanta, Georgia. Philip would have to care for our daughters while also working his full-time shift at the post office. This would surely add more pressure on him. But I knew my oldest daughters would be fine. It was Chante' I worried about. She was still a baby and required extra care. I was relieved when Mama stepped in and offered to care for Chante'. So, I sent her to Jamaica.

One challenge resolved—many more to come.

When I began the training, I realized it would be no walk in the park. The job was intense. The training spared no one. On my second day, one of the trainers even made a remark I will never forget. "I don't think you're going to make it," said Blanca, a company veteran who had trained hundreds of employees. I sat in shock. She had a keen eye for talent. Of course, it stung to hear her say those words. My failure had been predicted before I could start. Was she right?

I went home in tears, thinking of the sacrifices and hard work I put forth just to hear those words. I had to train in another state, send my baby out the country, and spent more time away from my other children. All while trying to process new skills and concepts for this company. I put so much on the line for this opportunity; I didn't even consider what would happen if it didn't work. Blanca's doubts made me take a moment to reflect and pray. *Lord, give me the knowledge to learn and the strength to endure.*

The next day, I returned to my job with a new surge of energy. My mind felt renewed. I realized Blanca's words were a test of my endurance and trust in God. It wasn't a time to surrender, but a time to believe. I affirmed myself, "I can make it. I just need more time and more focus." With my new attitude, I found myself learning and growing in every aspect of the job.

I kept this up beyond training and received great feedback from customers. My dedication did not go unnoticed by my supervisors.

"A great employee at such a difficult job."

Funny enough, I became friends with Blanca later on. She was aware of my performance rating. So, we turned her negative words into a joke between us. "Remember when you told me I would never make it?"

Joking aside, I still felt unhappy with the number of challenges I faced in the company. On the surface, I was pleased with my success and happy with the pay and perks. But inside, there was a feeling of doubt on whether I could stay for the long term. The stress would eventually take its toll.

Church on Saturday mornings wasn't the same. I had Kameisha and Nekeisha, but one person was missing. My precious baby, Chante'. She was still more than seven hundred miles away with Mama. And though I knew she was in good hands, I missed her. I felt guilty and sad for sacrificing this time with her. The only way I could cope with her absence was to keep my mind focused on the goal at hand – a promotion at work. I needed advanced skills to get me there. I was on the right path; I just needed to stay the course. I was hurting without my daughter, but I knew God would be with me every step of the way.

~

ENDURANCE.

This seemed to be the theme of my life. It was no different at my job. There was stress from customers. Negativity from coworkers. But I did what I do best – endured. For eight long years. When I finally decided I was ready to leave, it wasn't because I couldn't handle the challenges. Any job worth having comes with its ups and downs. I learned all I could. It was the most advanced position I had held thus far. But an old yearning crept up within me.

My educational pursuit was on my mind once again. I wanted to move forward with obtaining my bachelor's degree, and having it would open the door to more upper-level positions. Customer service wasn't my endgame. It was time to move up into a managerial role.

"You must be crazy!" I wish I could count all the times I heard this from coworkers when they found out I was going back to college. "How in the world can you juggle it all?"

"I have a plan to get out of here," I told them.

"Oh, c'mon," one would say. Another would scoff: "With this salary and benefits? Are you gonna walk out on a corporate job a lot of people dream of and never get? Never. You're not going anywhere!"

But I was. I deserved to take advantage of one of our perks: tuition reimbursement. After all of the stress from the job, the least they could do was pay for my education. So, I decided to begin a management program at Barry University. Working by day. Studying by night. Caring for my husband and children whenever I could pull myself away. I had to make it happen. I took two classes a semester. There were countless late nights of running in to check the kids' homework and then working on my own. The pressure to excel was also on my back. Barry had high academic standards. The journey was not comfortable. But my determination never wavered. It all paid off on September 20, 1998. The day I received my Bachelor of Science in Management.

I did it!

With the help of God, *we* did it!

We had to celebrate! My family threw a party in my honor. Even family and loved ones from Jamaica flew out for the occasion. The decorations. The cake. They were all reminders of what I had accomplished after a tough journey. I wore my graduation gown as I walked into the living room filled with beaming guests. Clapping and cheering. It dawned on me. I had just become the *only* member of my family to complete a four-year college program. This was historic for us! Though they were back in Jamaica, my parents were ecstatic. I remembered Mama's words so many years before, "Go forward, and chase your dreams. The doors that were closed to me are opening to you."

"I want to express my gratitude for a rewarding professional association during my employment." I was ready to hand in my resignation letter to my manager. "This decision was not an easy one and involved many hours of thoughtful consideration, particularly concerning my plans for the future. I am confident, however, that I have made a positive move toward fulfilling my career goals."

After typing up that letter, I went straight to the supervisor's office.

"Can I speak to you?" I said.

She looked up from her computer.

"Yes, of course," she said. "Come in." I could tell she had no idea what I was going to say.

"I've decided to resign."

"What?!"

My manager was a kind lady who I respected. She listened to my reasons and understood why I had to move on. She wished me well. I went back to my desk and stacked all my belongings in a box. The day was May 12, 2000. My time there was over. A bold move this was. I was ready for a new chapter in my life. I came to the realization a higher position wasn't in the future for me at this company. A promotion would have forced me to relocate to Atlanta. With Philip's job and our family in Florida, moving to another state was out of the question.

I also knew in my heart I could do better than spending forty hours a week locked into a cubicle. Attached to a phone. Only one problem. I didn't know what "better" was. I thought maybe I wasn't going to find it until I went looking. So, I took the plunge to resign.

Before I left, my main concern was Philip's reaction. I was walking away from good pay and benefits. I would be making a decision that would affect the entire family. To see how he would feel, I told him I resigned before I turned in my letter. Yes, I faked it.

"Philip, I went into work today," I said, "and I *resigned*."

"Oh, okay," he said.

A few moments pass before he says anything else.

"Guess you have to find something else to do."

The conversation was over. No shock. No angry words.

This was the extra push I needed. If Philip lost his cool, I would have to reconsider my decision. But his reaction meant he listened to all of my stressful stories. He knew this job was beginning to chip away from my creativity and talent. Philip understood just as much as I did how confining corporate America was becoming for me. With the experience I had running a company, I had what it took to make decisions, analyze results, and strategize follow-up plans. My husband saw this in me. He believed I was capable of more. *I* believed I was capable of more.

Looking back on the waters, I feel a sense of peace knowing the Captain has changed the course. A better path has been created for our voyage. A bigger discovery will be prepared at our destination.

Deck 6

DUTY-FREE: CHANGING DIRECTIONS

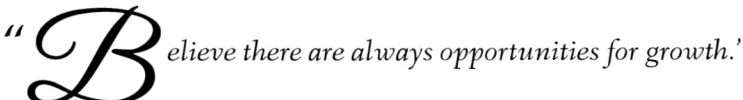

"*Believe there are always opportunities for growth.*"

THE STORMS HAVE SLIGHTLY CALMED. THE WATERS HAVE slowed. I can see the sky beginning to clear as the clouds return to a light hue of gray. I feel the calmness return to the ship as our spirits start to settle.

Our new course has brought on many new challenges, but we're still flowing along at normal speed. Anxious to see what the journey brings next.

LEAVING MY PREVIOUS JOB MEANT MORE THAN JUST "quitting." For me, this signified my rejection of corporate America. Decades later, I see why it was difficult for me to be in a role where I was just looking for my next paycheck. I didn't mind performing the daily tasks assigned to me. But I've always desired more. I had an enterprising spirit I wanted to put to the test.

Pastor Gray's words stuck with me as I moved forward. I could succeed at whatever I set my mind to because I always found a way to overcome obstacles. It came naturally for me. God gave me many talents. I never stopped believing in them. I refused to take another job just for the money and allow myself to be stifled. My plans were higher. I wanted to go higher up the educational ladder. My sights were set on an advanced degree to expose myself to even more knowledge. A few Google searches later; I found an MBA program at the University of Phoenix. The next step was to decide on a focus for the program.

Everything about my professional and educational background pointed in the managerial direction. I noticed the world around me becoming more digital. Computers were driving change in all industries. The door was opening for businesses to tap into global markets for growth. With these facts in mind, I landed on global management as my area of study. What better way to become marketable for more opportunities!

Graduate-level studies were more difficult than I had imagined. I was prepared to increase my level of learning. But I wasn't as privy to how challenging it would be. As I reflect on my course load during those days, I am thankful I didn't have to balance the program AND a full-time job. School required me to spend all day and almost all night to research and write detailed reports. When I wasn't performing my wifely and motherly duties, I was writing and taking assessments. I managed to do this until December 2003, when I was awarded a Master of Business Administration with a concentration in Global Management. Another significant goal accomplished! Our daughters planned an amazing graduation party amongst family and friends to celebrate this wonderful achievement!

While we were celebrating, my motivation to go back to school and further my education had somehow reignited my husband's interest to do the same. I had always known Philip regretted not having completed a four-year degree. My educational pursuit gave him the push to try again. When I committed myself to a consistent regimen of focused study, Philip was observing the entire time. "Why not pursue a bachelor's in postal management?" I suggested. Philip already had an associate degree from Miami Dade Community College. Taking this next step would only require two more years of study. Even though he was working full-time at the post office, Philip managed to complete the program. In September 2005, he received Bachelor of Arts degree in Business Management! It felt great knowing my love of learning had encouraged my husband to obtain a higher degree also. Nothing could have pleased me more.

MANY STEPS TO A BETTER FUTURE

On top of receiving my bachelor's and master's degrees, I had decades of work experience in a country with one of the world's largest economies. I felt so proud of myself! But my Jamaican roots lived in the forefront of my mind. I never forgot I had to leave my country just to get ahead. I knew many young people in Jamaica were still facing the same difficult choice. So, when a friend from church invited me to be part of a start-up with the potential to provide jobs for thousands of young Jamaicans, I was all ears.

Patrick and I met at church about five years before. Through casual conversations, I told him about my experience with managing Kenneth's business. Patrick was impressed with the knowledge and skillset I had developed over time. "You have great leadership qualities and organizational skills," he said.

He began to tell me about a call center he was planning to open in Jamaica. The center, CayTech, would provide customer service clientele or management staff from India. He invited me to join him in getting CayTech up and running. I would first have to teach the trainer the ins and outs, and then train the customer service representatives. The idea appealed to me because of my heart for helping the people of my home country. So, I gladly accepted.

I was not prepared for what was ahead of us. My first task was challenging. I was asked to write a call center manual. To write the manual, I first reviewed information from the trainers in India to confirm they were on the right track. Afterward, I had to dive into a list of call center training resources I generated from an online search. Launching the business was no easy job either. We depended on receiving funds from the Jamaican government. Their assistance would allow us to build out the call center and train hundreds of young Jamaicans. We planned and planned. Unfortunately, the funds never came through. Eventually, the project died.

I was devastated just thinking of all those hopeful young Jamaicans who were let down. They hungered for the most essential things most people tend to take for granted. A steady paycheck would've helped to support themselves, feed their children, and improve their parents' lives. They were trapped in a country where being unemployed limited what they could achieve. Even if they graduate high school at the top of their class, they're still not expected to find a decent job. My heart was crushed thinking of this.

But something good did come from the CayTech project years after it failed. Kenneth, my brother, who had been involved with the original start-up, was intrigued by the idea of providing jobs for many people. He pitched the idea to a local bank and secured a loan! From there, he built a state of the art call center in Mandeville, Jamaica.

I'm happy to say, the call center is still going strong today. It employs over three thousand Jamaicans! This project was a big step in what has become a significant investment in Jamaica's future.

I'm not surprised this cruise is taking unexpected detours.

Such is life.

My trust is not in the GPS, but the Captain who's leading the ship. My next move may be uncertain, but my *Guide's* direction isn't.

Deck 7

SHORE EXCURSIONS: CREATING MY OWN PATHWAY

"*Whatever things you ask when you pray, Believe that you receive them, and you will have them*," (*Mark 11:24*).

AFTER SPENDING SO MUCH TRAVEL TIME ANXIOUSLY, awaiting my next step, it feels nice to breathe. Knowing the Captain is making the path clear again gives me the chance to enjoy the breeze sweeping through my hair. The sun kissing my skin. The beautiful views of the shore in my background. Let's explore.

WHAT NOW?

The next steps in my career path weren't entirely clear after the Caytech project fell apart. Then my husband shared an idea with me. "Why don't we open a real estate company?" He knew going back to Corporate America was out of the question. He could feel I was ready for a fresh new challenge. Philip's father introduced him to the business of real estate through his success in buying and maintaining rental properties. Intrigued with the ins and outs of the market, Philip decided to get his license in 1999.

It didn't take long for his interest to rub off on me, especially since our first home purchase turned a profit twice its worth. In the early nineties, we invested in our second property – a four-plex in North Miami. It brought a very nice return when we sold it a few years ago. Seeing the fruits of our investments led us to think, could we turn our hobby into a full-time business?

There were many factors to consider. Market conditions. Owner experience. Industry outlook. I did what I do best – research. The market was on steady ground and described by some experts as *vibrant*. Everything seemed to be aligned, even our timing. Although I didn't have a steady job, we still had Philip's full-time salary and benefits from the post office to fall back on should our new business take a turn for the worst. It was time to put our plans in motion.

The first step for me was to get my real estate license. No problem. I obtained it in 2004 in a matter of months. Next, I needed guidance on setting up a real estate business. Philip wanted to be involved, but he was limited by his long work hours. So, I turned to Google. I learned all the legal details to ensure my license was appropriately registered. The final hurdle was securing an office space. I had no experience in this area, but I knew what the perfect space required for us both. As soon as I found the right building in Miramar, FL, I signed a one-year lease, and we were ready to go!

HOMEVALUE REALTY, LLC (*NOW KNOWN AS THE HomeValue Group*).

I came up with this name with our mission in mind: *to help first-time buyers realize the American Dream through what is usually the biggest purchase of anyone's life - a home.* "Making your real estate dreams a reality," was our philosophy.

The exciting part came when it was time to spruce up the office space. We installed computers, desks, a copier, and phones. Once we got everything set up, there was only one problem. The business didn't pick up right away. The entire first year was slow. Maybe we just needed a little more exposure, I thought. I hit the ground running and started handing out business cards everywhere I went. I made sure all our friends and acquaintances knew I'd become a real estate agent. I even reached out to banks. If they needed help with a Broker Price Opinion (BPO), I knew how to write appraisals for properties in their portfolios.

Little by little, things picked up. More BPO requests came in. I was able to hire our first employee, David, who helped me finalize the BPOs I was submitting to the banks. In addition to the BPOs, I started to focus on foreclosure listings and noticed our revenue expanding. I could finally see our hard work paying off. Our business investment was growing. This was a relief after spending a full year wearing many hats – human resources manager, payroll specialist, advertiser, marketing coordinator, and yes, even receptionist. Long gone were the days when I could clock out at 5 p.m. My workdays had no end. However, this brought me so much fulfillment. Our business was my pride and joy.

"I've made it," I told myself. "I'm doing exactly what I envisioned all those years ago at my other companies. I don't ever have to be a corporate zombie again. Whatever it takes to keep the business going, I'll do, knowing God will bless my efforts. His guidance will see me through."

There were 60,000 licensed and experienced real estate agents in the tri-county area. All no further than a few miles away from potential customers. What was going to make The HomeValue Group stand out?

I lost a lot of sleep during those early years, trying to figure out the *secret weapon* to conquer success. My initial thought was to beat every competitor in customer service. But with a steady market and content buyers and sellers, there was little to no opportunity to showcase this. It would nearly take a real estate collapse. In 2007, it was tough to predict how a market decline would impact our young business. Would we have a chance to shine, or would we plummet also?

Little did we know, we would soon find out. In 2008, the housing market crashed.

My company wasn't immune to the spiraling downfall caused by the massive dip in the national economy. Transactions were coming to a halt. I had to lay off an employee. Many brokers decided to close their companies. Several agents were running back to Corporate America. The chaos was unbelievable.

I had a choice. Do I join them and return to my safety net career? Or do I stand firm and fight for the business I grew to love? Although the odds were stacked against me, I chose to fight it out. Even during a crisis, I developed a plan of action. I realized a flaw in our original plan – we were too narrowly focused for such dire times. Our target audience, mostly first-time buyers, were now wiped from our focus. More attention needed to be placed on those who were in danger of losing their homes.

WE WERE LIVING IN DESPERATE TIMES. BANKS BEGAN TO encourage homeowners to sell for less than the amount owed on their mortgages. It was a tactic to recoup as much loan revenue as possible. These transactions were known as "short sales." I soon saw them take place within my own business. Was it risky? Absolutely.

This opportunity could save us from drowning. So, I went for it. The real estate board sponsored workshops for any realtor who wanted to learn more about short sales. Could this process be the insurance policy I needed to keep my business afloat? I was open. So, I attended *every* workshop within a fifty-mile radius of Miramar. I studied the handouts, front to back – over and over again. When I returned to my office, I was anxious to apply everything I had learned. It took me a while to get the hang of it, but I didn't give up.

I started by approaching every client on the path towards foreclosure and broke the news. "Don't fool yourselves into thinking the bank won't foreclose," I said. "It's not a far-fetched idea. It's a reality you must face." As fear grew in their eyes, I could not imagine the sadness they felt. But I had a job to do. Emotions could not cloud their judgment or my own. They needed someone who gave them a solid plan to move forward. I was just the person.

"Don't let a foreclosure ruin your credit for years to come," I told them. "If the bank approves, let's do a short sale. The bank waives the difference between what you owe and what the home's value is right now. A short sale doesn't count against you. Wait a little bit; then you can buy again. And don't you worry; I'm here to help."

I must've repeated this hundreds of times. I slowly transitioned into a consultant and a real estate owned (REO) and certified distressed property expert (CDPE). The career growth I was hoping for! Philip and I were hired to be consultants on foreclosed properties for the city of Miami Gardens Neighborhood Stabilization Program (NSP). In time, we won a huge contract with the federal government, operating out of Fort Lauderdale. This opportunity was followed by contracts with other reputable departments within the state. Our business continued to bloom beyond our imaginations.

Growth came with the challenge of learning how to resolve tough client situations. "How long haven't you paid your mortgage?" I would ask the clients. Some would say three months while needing another month or two to catch up. I learned early on how hard it could be for clients to catch up with payments. Ultimately, they were in the most danger of losing their homes. It was tough having to simply nod at them when inside, I knew what had to be done.

I learned to handle some of the most delicate situations. Unfortunately, many mortgage holders were in denial of what was happening. It takes me back to the day when I had to travel to a foreclosed property with a few sheriff deputies. A woman owned the home, but she was not there at the moment. The deputies opened the door with the intent to remove her items. As I looked around, I noticed the intricate details. This family's life was evident. There were a refrigerator and cabinets fully stocked with groceries. Family photos lined the walls. You could still smell the breakfast she prepared earlier that morning, and see its remnants remaining on the stove. All I could think of was a tired woman coming home from a long day of work to find her house completely bolted. Her belongings piled on the front lawn if they hadn't been stolen by then. My heart broke at the thought.

I wasn't sure if I could do anything to stop this from happening. But I had to try. I asked the deputies to move on to the next property while I tried to get in touch with the woman. I knocked on her neighbor's door, convinced them to give me her number, and dialed her as quickly as I could. Thankfully, I reached her. "What in the world are you talking about?" she said. "I can't get there now. I'm *at work!*" I let out a sigh of hopelessness. But I couldn't just hang up. I explained the entire situation to her again. She was able to tell her manager it was an emergency and made it just in time with a moving truck to get her things. "I don't know how to thank you," she said to me with tears in her eyes.

My personal and professional goal was to handle each owner with this same level of compassion. Losing one's home was hard enough. I wanted to at least help them walk out with dignity.

This level of customer service sparked the word around town about our business. The people I helped shared their experiences with others! In my eyes, the key to success for HomeValue Realty went beyond profit. It was all about having a charitable spirit. Helping people find and keep a home they could afford. I learned this value from the best – my Mama. She couldn't deny food to neighbors who had no money to pay. And I couldn't deny the chance to help a client close a deal, even if it meant giving up my commission.

Fifteen years later, Philip and I are still going strong with a team of ten! We are still offering the kind of customer service people take note of, even by big names in the industry. We've had the chance to learn from leading real estate franchisers while growing our business model. Our daughter, Chante', has joined us as our Team Lead. She brings such a robust and energetic spirit to the team. We are watching our business elevate to levels of success even I did not expect!

This path has brought new success. New growth. My excursion was filled with new beginnings and great views. We're sailing on now...

Deck 8

CRUISIN' ON TO HIGHER DEGREES

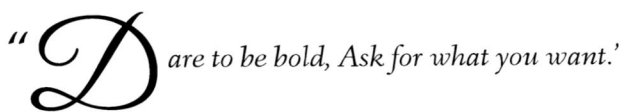

"WELCOME BACK, PASSENGERS! WE'RE PREPARING TO CRUISE on to our destination. Enjoy the rest of your trip."

Hearing the Captain call for us brings great excitement as I gear up for the rest of the voyage. What will the sea be like now? Will the skies remain clear? I'll have to stay the course to find out.

...and we're cruising.

IT WAS TIME TO TAKE ANOTHER LOOK AT MY LIFE. WAS THERE more? Was I missing something? It had been five years since we opened the realty business. In 2011, business was booming. The number of short sales we had already handled brought in very nice profits. We also gained excellent name recognition in the tri-county area. Breaking even was no longer our concern.

However, I wasn't fulfilled. Life meant more to me than money and careers. While I was satisfied professionally, my spiritual being needed more. My mind always went back to the summer job I had when I was younger, working with Jamaicans who lived in impoverished areas. Now, I was also thinking of the troubled homeowners I was coaching through the worst financial crisis of their lives. I just knew there had to be a way for me to help them. I was being called for a great *work*. It was time to fulfill a lifelong desire to give back to those around me.

I decided to couple this with my other dream to continue pursuing higher education. I wanted to take my educational journey as far as it could go. There was a doctoral degree I knew would put me in the position to give back in a more significant way than before. So, I applied to Walden University's Ph.D. program in the field of Human Services.

Here I was pursuing another passion while running a business and taking care of my family. Although I knew this meant developing another tiresome schedule, I had to make it happen. My daily routine began at 4 a.m. I had to start my studies early. I would continue researching and writing after work until about midnight. My Sabbath was observed from Friday evening at sunset to Saturday evening at sunset. Although I maintained this strict schedule throughout my time in school, I had moments of wanting to give up.

Life took a toll on me during this journey. My dear sister, Jean, died suddenly from a heart attack. Losing her was an extreme heartbreak for me. I remember confiding in a friend and classmate, Dr. Maryse Desir, because the grief and stress became too much to bear. Dr. Desir was the moral support I needed to get me through such tough times. So, I managed to stay the course.

MY ACADEMIC JOURNEY TOOK MANY TWISTS AND TURNS. BUT

ultimately, I gained a lot of insight and experience from the program. Although I aced all my advanced coursework, I entered the dissertation phase with some apprehension. This was going to be the largest piece of work in fulfilling my doctoral degree. However, this project fueled my passion even more. My topic was centered around children in foster care. I felt my energy become more propelled chapter by chapter. I gained many new insights along the way, learning more about how to successfully become the change I wanted to see.

After spending much time on data collection, analysis, practical applications, and more, I was more versed on this topic than ever before. My studies revealed possible and realistic solutions for mitigating negative outcomes of the foster care experience. I also discovered the potential to create positive social change by engaging all stakeholders in the effort to improve the well-being and future for youth in foster care. My wheels were turning for social issues, even beyond this topic. I knew I made the right decision to pursue this degree.

You can imagine the excitement I felt when I read, "Congratulations!" in the email subject heading I received on February 27, 2017. *"The Chief Academic Officer (CAO) has approved your dissertation as meeting Walden University's high standards of academic rigor. You should be very proud of your accomplishment, and we look forward to soon celebrating your achievement at an upcoming commencement."* My dissertation, "Exploring Social Support Networks of African American Emancipated Foster Care Women," was completed in eleven months, breaking the twelve-month record set by a former student.

Graduation Day was finally here. July 12, 2017. There was not a cloud in sight. The sun shined brightly as if it were celebrating me too! I will never forget the day. My family and friends were there to watch me walk across the stage and receive my hood. My mind was filled with thoughts of the challenges, determination, and perseverance it took to get there. Filled with joy, I smiled as the university's president announced to our class, "You have earned the highest degree in your field of study." I remembered being told the work would be too rigorous. I wouldn't be able to do it. But I believe anything is possible. *You* just have to believe.

As waves of thoughts continued to enter my mind, I decided to focus and let the moment sink in. From hearing my name called to seeing the proud smiles in the audience, it became real for me. I was officially awarded a Doctor of Philosophy in Human Services with a concentration in Family Studies and Intervention Strategies.

Without the constant love and care of my Lord and Savior, Jesus Christ, I would not have lived through this moment. He was my Rock and my Shield. He blessed me with a loving and supportive husband who spent late nights with me. Assisting me in my studies and taking care of the household. Our daughters even made Philip a t-shirt with the phrase, "I survived my wife's dissertation." No doubt about it!

I couldn't be more grateful for my Lord.

I couldn't be more grateful for my support system.

I couldn't be more grateful for achieving yet another milestone.

We're not always smooth sailing on this cruise, but we're journeying forward. I feel in my heart; the destination will make sense. I'm ready to keep cruisin' on.

Deck 9

A PECULIAR PENTHOUSE: ADVOCATING FOR CHANGE

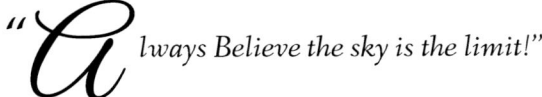

"*Always Believe the sky is the limit!*"

THE SHIP'S HORNS AWAKEN ME. I TAKE A LOOK AND SEE WE'RE closer to land. Finally, the destination is in near sight. My views from the penthouse are spectacular. I marvel at the blue waves. The sun kissing the tops of the tall buildings. What a beautiful picture, soon to be my reality.

GAINING ACADEMIC CREDENTIALS AND REAL ESTATE experience afforded many great opportunities. In 2018, I was appointed as one of the members of the City of Miramar Afford-able Housing Advisory Committee. I worked with other committee members to establish policy and procedures and implement afford-able housing strategies for residents of Miramar.

I received a teaching invitation from Broward College one fall morning in 2019. Boy, was I happy when I saw the email in my inbox! Two years earlier, I attended a career day at the school and left my resume. I never heard a word afterwards. I was a bit disappointed because I've always wanted to dive into teaching. I considered entering this career to be one of the best ways to make a difference. Once again, the Lord was showing me He could make my dreams come true.

THE YEAR 2020 HAS COME. ONE THING HAS REMAINED THE same about me. I am still looking for ways to give back. Fortunately, I've been able to do so through various ventures. On December 30, 2019, I was appointed by the Realtors of Greater Fort Lauderdale and the Palm Beaches as a committee member of the Community Outreach of Broward County. I am delighted to serve in this capacity as I am able to give back to people in need.

On January 12, 2020, I launched my nonprofit organization, Fostering Connections. My organization was motivated by my desire to help teenagers in foster care. I was fueled by the research I conducted while writing my doctoral dissertation on the topic. I also found inspiration in Betsy Krebs, a lawyer who founded a youth advocacy center in New York. Since our launch, Fostering Connections has had the opportunity to partner with an elementary school in Manchester, Jamaica. Our goal is to provide clothing and school supplies to underprivileged children in South Manchester. It warms my heart knowing I will be able to give back to the same area where my mom grew up.

I'm not sure what I imagined the destination to be like, but this was much better. I can't believe it. I made it. I am here. The Captain kept me. I have arrived.

Deck 10

DEBARKATION: REFLECTING ON THE JOURNEY

"*Believe that God is good, He will carry you through the most difficult challenges in your life.*"

As I plant my feet on fresh soil, all I can think is, "Thank you, Captain." I thank Him for safety, provision, and comfort during my journey to this new land. Waves crashed against us. Storms threatened our course. But He steered me to where I needed to be. Safe and sound.

To *believe* is to hold confidence and trust in a person or concept. I believe in God. I believe in His strength. I believe He can do the impossible. I believe He can open doors no one can shut and shut doors no one can open. I believe if I work hard, if I remain committed, and if I am determined, then I can achieve all the benefits of a prosperous life. A young country girl believed she was destined to be successful. She knew anything was possible, and the mind was a terrible thing to waste. I took on enormous challenges and risks, which cemented my stance on believing in my dreams.

I am now at the beginning of a new phase of my life — one in which I am destined to give back to foster care children in the United States. I am also committed to underserved children and families in Jamaica and other parts of the world. My goal is to teach others to get involved. My husband, Philip, remains excellent support, and my daughters are all adults making a positive impact in their chosen careers. I can say, without a doubt, I am blessed.

The summer job I was assigned over forty years ago was the starting point to where I am today. I must do what I am called to do. I must make a positive impact on who I am called to serve. I must encourage others to do the same. For me, believing is purposefully and intentionally making a difference in the lives of others.

Believing is never about giving up on yourself but trusting your abilities. You have to know you can achieve anything if you *believe*. This is faith. I saw it in my parents – in the way they taught my brothers and sisters to believe in God and trust everything is possible with Him. For my Papa, a hard worker and committed family man who provided for his children. For my Mama, a sweet and caring person, rooted in her beliefs who stood firm in her Christian principles.

In sharing my story, I hope to help someone believe in all the blessings the Lord has for them. I have been blessed to have a wonderful God, a loving family, and fantastic role models in my life. For every opportunity opened for me, I intend to share the space with anyone willing to be involved. There is power in blending our voices in unique ways to bring authentic volume to things we believe. Becoming advocates for social change is possible if we *believe*.

"Therefore, I say unto you, whatever things you ask

when you pray, believe that you receive them,
and you will have them." Mark 11:24

    I do not know when the next journey will begin and where it will take me. But I do know with my Captain, any destination is possible. With Him, I will continue to cruise on and see where the ship of life takes us next.

Made in the USA
Middletown, DE
23 November 2025

22421705R00062